simon & schuster

new york

london

toronto

sydney

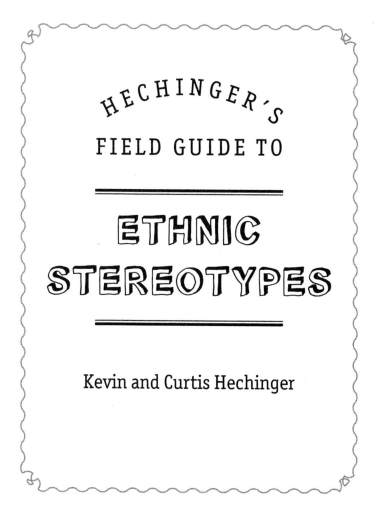

HECHINGER'S
FIELD GUIDE TO

ETHNIC STEREOTYPES

Kevin and Curtis Hechinger

Simon & Schuster Paperbacks
A Division of Simon & Schuster, Inc.
1230 Avenue of the Americas
New York, NY 10020

First Simon & Schuster trade paperback edition February 2009

SIMON & SCHUSTER PAPERBACKS and colophon are registered trademarks
of Simon & Schuster, Inc.

For information about special discounts for bulk purchases,
please contact Simon & Schuster Special Sales at
1-800-456-6798 or business@simonandschuster.com.

Designed by Diane Hobbing of Snap-Haus Graphics

Manufactured in the United States of America

10   9   8   7   6   5   4   3   2   1

Library of Congress Cataloging-in-Publication Data

Hechinger, Kevin.
    Hechinger's field guide to ethnic stereotypes / Kevin and Curtis Hechinger.
        p. cm.
    1. Ethnology—Humor. 2. Stereotypes (Social psychology)—Humor.
I. Hechinger, Curtis. II. Title.
    PN6231.E78H43 2009
    818'.607—dc22

                                    2008038727

ISBN-13: 978-1-4165-7782-9
ISBN-10:   1-4165-7782-3

For Alicia.
—Kevin

To Greg, for everything.
—Curtis

CONTENTS

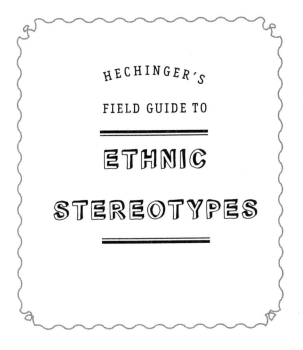

HECHINGER'S

FIELD GUIDE TO

ETHNIC

STEREOTYPES

CHAPTER I

INTRODUCTION

Half an hour ago you ordered some Chinese food. Now there's a knock on the door and someone's shouting, "Delivery!" As you open the door, what do you expect to see? If your answer is "A skinny, young Asian man with a wispy mustache and a bag of Chinese food," then chances are you're dead wrong. Recent research indicates that Asians rarely deliver Chinese food anymore. Most of them have gotten so good at math they go directly from high school to the research and analysis department at Goldman Sachs.

If you live in the New York tristate area, there's an 80 percent probability that your Chinese food will be delivered by a Senegalese man who claims to have been a doctor back in his native land but who, in truth, delivered food there, too. (This deliveryman is an archetypal representation of a burgeoning new ethnic stereotype: the Incomprehensible but Highly Opinionated African.)

But this fascinating paradigm transformation isn't just limited to the world of take-out food. The emotion required to navigate the complex waters of our shifting national ethnicity can affect our very democracy. In fact, many political analysts say that John Kerry actually lost the 2004 election during a whistle-stop tour through Florida when he visited a Broward County bar and ordered a Thug's Passion. (See chapter 2 for the recipes to this and other popular Black cocktails.)

A massive and fundamental change has occurred in the anthropological landscape of North America, and *Hechinger's Field Guide to Ethnic Stereotypes* will help you navigate the new, culturally rocky terrain. Eight years ago our grandfather Karl Hechinger started this field guide with a dual mission. Through exhaustive research and empirical evidence he wanted to document how ethnic "types" are really not all that different from one another. Sure, the Polish eat *pierogis* and the Japanese eat *gyoza,* but when you get right down to it . . . a stuffed dumpling is a stuffed dumpling. Like it or not, we are all more alike than we care to admit.

Grampa Karl also anticipated the need for a guide to the exploding ethnic melting pot in which we're living. North America is home to people from 168 different countries. So, the old stereotypes simply don't apply anymore. The rules have changed and we need a new playbook.

Unfortunately, Grampa was only halfway finished with this edition when tragedy struck. He was shot to death by a couple of crack-addled Jamaicans who broke into his apartment. (For more information on Drug-Addled Jamaicans, please turn to chapter 2; recipes for jerk chicken and homemade crystal meth follow.)

Grampa's dream became our mission. We visited every corner of this great land. We got shot at by territorial lobstermen in Maine, did shots of cobra's blood with Vietnamese mechanics in Detroit, and got hepatitis shots from a Guatemalan internist in Orange County. We saw every style, color, brand, blend, creed, and hue of every man, woman, child, nut bag, and whack job this majestic land has to offer. We learned many lessons, perhaps none more important than *never drink cobra's blood.*

Hechinger's Field Guide to Ethnic Stereotypes is an invaluable tool for the professional cultural anthropologist as well as the amateur enthusiast. In the pages that follow you will learn a lot about this land we all call home. You'll also learn a lot about yourselves.

CHAPTER II

BLACKS

Throughout this book we will be using plain language to talk about complicated subjects. Blacks, Browns, Whites, and Yellows are just general terms that allow us to delve into the fascinating subsets that exist within all ethnic groups. But it's important that we define our terms as precisely as possible.

So, for the "Black" chapter, let's set the record straight: *African-American* refers to descendants of those who came from Africa. Therefore, Blacks can be African-Americans, but they're not *only* African-Americans. Blacks can also hail from countries such as Haiti and Jamaica. These folk generally refer to themselves as Haitian-Americans or Jamaican-Americans as opposed to African-Americans—although the Blacks in Haiti and Jamaica came from Africa originally, too. It sounds confusing, but when you factor in the fact that everyone on the planet probably came from Africa to begin with, it all kind of evens itself out.

Coloreds is not used anymore except when recycling paper or doing the wash. *Negro* is pretty much only used in the United Negro College Fund. And don't even go near the other N-word. (See chapter 11 for our *Pocket Survival Guide*.)

Although things didn't exactly start out well for Blacks in this country, they are without a doubt key contributors to the essence of America. Black history is inextricably interwoven into the fabric of our nation. Perhaps that is why, to this day, Blacks are still associated with "the weave."

Without the "Black experience" we wouldn't have:

- Jazz
- Soul food
- *SportsCenter* highlights
- Something to keep White America from feeling guilty about wiping out the Indians

STEREOTYPES

Perhaps no other ethnic group has been so burdened by a variety of pervasive stereotypes. Addressing and debunking them may be the most effective way of wending a path through the fascinating rainbow of Black-ish ethnic permutations.

1. They are black

Untrue! Almost no Black people are actually black. Even Wesley Snipes is more of a rich, chocolaty-brown-with-dark-hints-of-mahogany accents than black-black. Perhaps the only truly black person whom we met in our extensive travels was an African-American named Barry from West Virginia. And his profound blackness may have been augmented by his having spent the past twenty-five years working in a coal mine.

2. They are better athletes

Untrue! Blacks are not better athletes than other ethnic groups. They're simply better athletes at the sports in which they are interested. For example, Blacks don't excel at water polo or lacrosse—primarily because Blacks don't usually play water polo or lacrosse. However, if Blacks do start playing water polo or lacrosse, then preppy White kids from Long Island better start figuring out a new way to get into Ivy League colleges.

3. They all talk funny

Untrue! Black culture has added enormously to the richness and complexity of our vocabulary and language. This opinion is universally accepted—except by linguists. Here's a brief look at some of the Black contributions to English.

A. Common Greetings and Salutations
- Yo.
- Whazzup? (This greeting was co-opted by advertising agencies in the nineties and is now solely used by pathetic "wiggers.")
- What it do, Shorty?
- What did I do, Officer?

B. New Words
- Rizzle/Snizzle/Shizzle (Or, really, anything with an -izzle at the end of it. We're not even sure if drizzle and sizzle have retained their original meanings.)
- Aks (as in "Did I aks you that already?")
- Aks (as in "Shit, 5-0 be bustin' in our door with they aks, yo!")

C. New Dialects
More significantly than introducing new words or phrases, Black America has generated its own linguistic dialect called Ebonics or AAV (African-American Vernacular).

Example:

"I aks Ruf wa she gwan ovah Tom crib."

Translation: "I asked Ruth if she was going over to Tom's apartment."

(Interesting side note: Ebonics has a great deal in common with the dialect spoken by Southern White Trash, who would also say, "I aks Ruf wa she gwan ovah Tom crib." The only difference in meaning would be that the SWT asked Ruth if she was going over to where Tom lay snoozing in a wooden baby crib, no doubt sleeping off a wicked moonshine bender.)

4. They are better lovers
Untrue! Blacks are not better lovers than other ethnic groups. The Orvis Study of 2001 didn't even discover a discernibly larger average penis size in African-American males. Although, surprisingly, Latinos turned out to have the largest testicles.

Perhaps this romantic stereotype has stuck so firmly because Black people aren't offended by it. Much like the ridiculous canard that Asians are smart or Jews are good with money, when the stereotype is positive, the stereotyped tend to encourage it.

5. They can't do anything with their hair
Untrue! While Black people's hair may be slightly less manageable than the hair of other ethnic groups, it has spawned a massive cottage industry in gels, sprays, chemical processes, and sticky unguents all geared toward doing something special with that 'do. Also, when all else fails, there's no shame in getting your weave on.

HECHINGER'S STYLE GUIDE TO FEMALE BLACK HAIRDOS

THE "SHE'S GOT TO HAVE IT"

THE "SUPERFLY"

THE "SHAFT"

THE "BINGO LONG TRAVELING ALL STARS"

THE "ROOTS"

THE "FISH THAT SAVED PITTSBURGH"

THE "CORNBREAD, EARL, & ME"

6. They all live in urban areas or the Deep South

Untrue! Only *most* Black people live in urban areas or the Deep South. Montel Williams lives in Greenwich, Connecticut.

Although most Blacks originally came from Africa to the Southeastern United States, we do not view this as a valid migratory episode because they didn't exactly have a say in the matter. By the late nineteenth century, Blacks had spread out quite a bit. The only place they seem not to have settled in is Wyoming, which is almost definitely all Dick Cheney's fault.

Although Black neighborhoods are basically the same as non-Black neighborhoods, there are some important distinctions.

In Black neighborhoods:

- Chinese restaurants serve fried chicken
- There is a 10:1 liquor-store-to-bank ratio
- There is a 1:1 beauty-salon-to-church ratio (and there are a lot of both)
- All the movie theaters provide an "interactive" experience
- At all retail establishments you have to talk through Plexiglass

Here are some things that you will generally *not* find in a Black neighborhood:

- Surfboards
- A Toyota Prius
- Scuba-diving equipment
- Rabbis

THUG'S PASSION DRINK RECIPE

1. *2 oz. Alizé liqueur*
2. *2 oz. Cristal Champagne*
3. *Mix over ice*
4. *Serve. Enjoy!*

THUG'S PASSION (PRISON VERSION)

1. *2 oz. prune juice fermented in toilet*
2. *4 oz. anything with fizz (Alka-Seltzer/Comet)*
3. *Add splash of lighter fluid*
4. *Serve over ice*
5. *Toss cellmate's salad and enjoy!*

7. They have funny names

Untrue! Black people have all kinds of names—only some of which are funny. As a rule, Blacks tend to be the most creative ethnicity when it comes to naming their offspring. Asians and Latinos are the least creative, using the same five or six names for roughly 4 billion people. Blacks, however, use references from Africa, colonial America, and the Benjamin Moore paint chart in the naming process. Then they scramble all that up in an elaborate naming machine akin to a particle accelerator, only more sophisticated. And that's how they spawn a variety of brand-new sobriquets.

If you would like to create an original Black name for yourself, follow the steps in the ensuing chart.

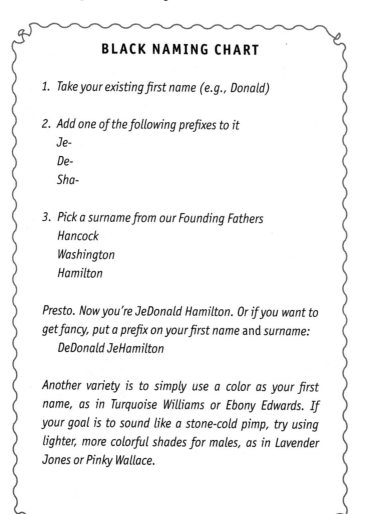

BLACK NAMING CHART

1. *Take your existing first name (e.g., Donald)*

2. *Add one of the following prefixes to it*
   Je-
   De-
   Sha-

3. *Pick a surname from our Founding Fathers*
   Hancock
   Washington
   Hamilton

Presto. Now you're JeDonald Hamilton. Or if you want to get fancy, put a prefix on your first name and surname:
   DeDonald JeHamilton

Another variety is to simply use a color as your first name, as in Turquoise Williams or Ebony Edwards. If your goal is to sound like a stone-cold pimp, try using lighter, more colorful shades for males, as in Lavender Jones or Pinky Wallace.

8. They're all cool

Untrue! While many Blacks are cool, and some—such as Miles Davis and Dave Chappelle—are cool enough to outcool entire other ethnicities all by themselves, not all Blacks are cool. In fact, the African-American Nerd is an increasingly common subtype. W. E. B. DuBois and Booker T. Washington were the first African-American Nerds (AANs). (FYI, Booker T. Washington is not to be confused with Booker T. and the M.G.'s, who actually are very cool.)

Some examples of the AAN:

- Cornel West
- Barack Obama
- Henry Louis Gates
- Condoleezza Rice
- Urkel (rumored to be the love child of Condoleezza and Cornel)

More Black Subsets

Haitian-Americans

Haitian-Americans are very misunderstood, primarily because they speak with a thick accent. In spite of their confusing way of talking, however, Haitian-Americans have high levels of achievement in academia. They are particularly successful in the field of geometry—probably because they have so much experience in triangulating gunfire to avoid revolutionary insurgents and government death squads.

Another fascinating tidbit about Haitian-Americans is that, no matter what they may say, they all believe in voodoo.

Jamaican-Americans

Jamaican-Americans are just like Haitian-Americans except they smoke a lot more pot. They are skilled at smoking the aforementioned pot, playing soccer, murdering rival gang members with machetes, and seducing the beautiful blond daughters of WASP businessmen. Having already invented a popular musical movement that combines spirituality with drug use, Jamaican-Americans are equally comfortable making music or drugs.

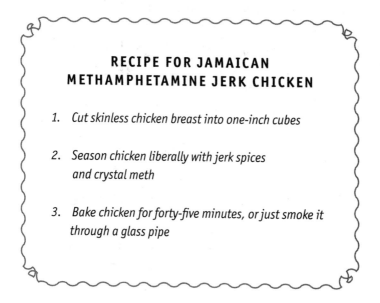

**RECIPE FOR JAMAICAN
METHAMPHETAMINE JERK CHICKEN**

1. *Cut skinless chicken breast into one-inch cubes*

2. *Season chicken liberally with jerk spices
   and crystal meth*

3. *Bake chicken for forty-five minutes, or just smoke it
   through a glass pipe*

(cont'd)

Like Haitian-Americans, Jamaican-Americans also speak with a thick accent. But their thick accent has been so overexposed on TV and in movies that everyone always knows what they're talking about. This accent is better known as a *patois*—pronounced *pa-twah* (or *pat-oyz* if you're a Stupid White Tourist from Ohio Hitting Montego Bay for Some Caribbean Fun and Cheap Weed (SWTFOHMBFSCFACW)).

Charismatic, Verbose Nigerian Cabdrivers

Primarily found in the greater Boston area, these extremely African African-Americans take the kooky accents to a whole new level. They will cheerfully describe "de Back Bay, mon" while taking an unnecessarily long route from Logan Airport to Faneuil Hall. Getting ripped off by a Nigerian Cabdriver isn't that bad, however. At least it's not as bad as getting ripped off by a Nigerian Internet Scammer. Take our advice: just because someone insists in an e-mail that they have $20 million in assets frozen by the government doesn't mean you should send an $800 check to some "lady" in Lagos.

The Black Urban Transvestite

Black Urban Transvestites (or BUTs) live predominantly in large urban areas such as New York, Los Angeles, and Detroit. Key West, Florida, also has a lot of BUTs. Their visual presentation is kind of like a cross between a top-notch professional athlete and a truck-stop stripper. Think Terrell Owens in fishnet stockings. Full of laughter and amusing asides, the Black Urban Transvestite is often the life of the party. Just remember not to get him mad—because he's as strong as an ox and probably has a blade hidden in his wig.

EAR PLUGS
DOUBLE AS
HOCKEY PUCKS

GOAT-MUFFS
AND THERMAL VESTS

QUILTED
DOWN-FILLED
DASHIKIS

WALKING STAFF-SKI POLE COMBO
GREAT FOR SCHUSHING AND
PRODDING THE LIVESTOCK

African New England Americans

Randy Moss isn't the only Black man to make the most of a New England winter. A small but hearty group of Africans who came from one of the hottest places on the face of the earth wound up in Lewiston, Maine. That's right—a large community of Somalians are living and looking for work in Maine. Not surprisingly, the In-bred Downeasters look at them as if they were Martians.

The community is thriving, however, and it's just a matter of time before the L.L. Bean catalog starts offering fleece head scarves and electric heated prayer rugs.

The Gangsta

Despite mounting evidence to the contrary, some African-Americans do actually commit crimes. The worst of these can be described as actual Gangstas. They really do all the heinous stuff that the Gangsta Rappers only rap about. While Gangstas and Gangsta Rappers have a great deal in common, there are some important distinctions between the two.

GOLD "GRILL" STOLEN FROM GANGSTA RAPPER

GOLD CHAINS PICKED UP FROM CORPSES

GUN— TO HURT HIS ENEMIES

BULLET HOLES— MADE BY ACTUAL BULLETS

SCAR— FROM KNIFE FIGHT AT RIKERS

The Gangsta Rapper

A growing subset, the Gangsta Rapper drives around in a shiny car, features shiny teeth, and raps about making mad shiny coin. Usually male, the Gangsta Rapper will often sport a moniker like Stone Kole Killa—but his real name is probably Morris or Leslie.

The Overeducated Militant Southern Female

Concentrated in larger Southern cities such as Atlanta (go to Dekalb Market on a Saturday and be prepared to get your ass and your shopping cart kicked), these women have a "my way or the highway" view of life. Arguably the only thing scarier than an angry Black Urban Transvestite is one of these ladies with a head of steam and a righteous cause.

To a Black male, seeing one of these women coming at you is scarier than seeing two White cops in your rearview mirror.

The Overeducated Militant Southern Female is strong, independent, and resourceful. Fiercely protective of family, she will scratch your eyes out if you look at her wrong.

Here are some warning signs that should let you know that whatever you just did or said, it was a big mistake, and now you're up shit creek:

- Hand on hip, which is shifted outward
- Eyes glaring with look of impending castration
- Slashing air with expertly painted and lethally long French nails
- Taking off enormous hoop earrings 'cause they just get in the way when it's ass-kicking time

If you experience two or more of these behavioral displays, you should immediately head for the nearest safety zone.

Tremendously Successful Celebrity/Athlete

To reach TSC/A status is the dream of all Americans (whether they're willing to admit it or not). For some reason, this state of überstardom is usually reserved for Blacks. Examples of this type:

- Oprah
- Michael Jordan
- Al Sharpton*

- Tiger Woods
- Will Smith

*We don't actually consider Al Sharpton to be that successful, but we felt we had to include him or he'd immediately stage a protest outside Simon & Schuster's NYC headquarters.

A subset of the Tremendously Successful Celebrity/Athlete is . . .

The Once Tremendously Successful Celebrity/Athlete Who Self-Destructed

Examples of this genus are:

- O. J. Simpson
- Michael Jackson
- Michael Vick
- Eddie Murphy (Okay, maybe Eddie didn't totally self-destruct. But he's Eddie Murphy, damn it! As funny as he used to be, it's criminal that now he only gets laughs when he's pulled over for giving rides to transvestites who probably have blades hidden in their wigs.)

The final subset of the TSC/A is the . . .

Tremendously Successful Celebrity/Athlete Who Self-Destructed but Miraculously Is Still Tremendously Successful

Examples of this group are:

- Clarence Thomas
- Kobe Bryant

- Ray Lewis
- Buckwheat

UNITED STATES

CHINOOKS

BEARS

BUFFALO

GRASS

CHUMASH

APACHES

MORE GRASS

PRAIRIE DOGS

GIANT ARMADILLOS

TUMBLE WEED

CIRCA 1500...

GIANT LOBSTERS

CAYUGAS

MOHICANS

POWHATANS

SWAMP

SPANIARDS

ALLIGATORS

MORE GIANT SWAMP

GIANT BUGS

GIANT SWAMP

CHAPTER III

BROWNS

While *Browns* refers to a large and diverse segment of the ethnic landscape, it also is the very first color of our country. This nation was birthed in Brown-ness and from Brown-ness it has flourished. Unless, of course, you consider American-Indians to be red . . . then we would have been birthed in Red-ness and we'd have to rethink this whole chapter. The seminal color study conducted by Dr. Maureen Havarti in 1974, however, clearly places the American-Indian in the Brown spectrum—so we shall press on.

Indians

The Indians were a peaceful group. For reasons that have never been determined, they turned bloodthirsty and savage after European settlers arrived and forced them off their own land after infecting them all with smallpox.

Given their common history of genocide, their fate is not unlike that of the Israelites—although we have yet to document any cases of a Jew actually talking to an Indian.

The two groups can be compared on many levels:

Indians enjoy camping outside.
Jews enjoy camps with Indian names.

Indians like natural foods.
Jews like Whole Foods.

Indians hunt and gather.
Jews order in.

Indians live on reservations.
Jews live for reservations.

Indians are deeply spiritual and embrace a pantheistic theology.
Jews run show business.

Names

Names are important to Indians, who strive for specificity and originality. Historically, American Indians named their offspring after nature: Meadow, River, Brook. But some names are earned in later life and are designed to reveal the essence of the individual's character. For example:

- Uncle Throws like a Girl
- Big Mama Thunder Thighs
- Chief Acorn Dick

In deference to modernity, many Native Americans now sport an "Anglo" first name and then an ancestral surname. For instance:

- Martin Running Deer
- Johnny Spear Beaver (not to be confused with Italian porn star Gianni Spear Beaver)

Geographical Dispersal

To this day, the vast majority of Indians live on reservations, except in Canada, where they are actually treated like human beings. (See *Hechinger's Field Guide to Ethnic Stereotypes—Canadian Edition*.)

Hundreds of reservations are scattered across this country, mostly on shitty, barren land, but the two basic types are:

Indian reservation without casino:

TYPE A -

TYPICAL INDIAN RESERVATION

Indian reservation with casino:

TYPE B -

TYPICAL INDIAN RESERVATION

Nesting Patterns

Although most think that tepees are an outmoded style of hous-
ing for Indians, the truth is that most of them do, in fact, live in
tepees. The only Indians who don't live in tepees are the ones who
got a piece of the casino money. They live in enormous tepees.

Behavioral Traits

Although most of us would be hard-pressed to distinguish between a Cherokee and a Seminole if we came across them at a
Baskin-Robbins, here's a quick tip on how to distinguish between
tribes:

- Apaches—angry
- Navajos—clever
- Seminoles—silly
- Shinnecocks—rowdy
- San Franciscos—gay

Occupations

• Pissed-Off College Mascot

Although political correctness has drastically reduced the work
options for Indians choosing this "career path," a number of Native American (NA) males and females are still making their living
dancing around sports arenas dressed like caricatures of their
ancestors.

- Chief Illiniwek (University of Illinois)
- Chief Wahoo (Cleveland Indians)
- The Binghamton Buffalo Fucker (proposed minor-league
  baseball team)

• High-Rise Construction Worker

No one knows why American Indians have a tolerance for working at such heights, but they have always used it to their advantage in securing these highly paid jobs. Unfortunately, they also always tend to blow their pay on cheap alcohol and expensive hookers. Coincidentally, that is the exact opposite of how the White construction worker blows his money.

• Indians

Surprisingly, being an Indian is one of the best jobs an Indian can get. Whether in a movie, on a TV show, or in a theme-park performance, professional-Indian Indians are raking in the wampum.

Natural Enemies

- Whites
- Disease-ridden blankets
- The IRS
- Steve Wynn
- Yosemite Sam
- Open bars

Common Misconceptions and Stereotypes

• They can't hold their alcohol

Actually, Indians hold their alcohol extremely well—in bottles, cans, empty plastic gasoline containers, even goat bladders. What they can't do is tolerate the alcohol once it's in their bodies.

• **They can communicate with wildlife**

Also untrue. American Indians often *try* to communicate with wildlife—especially when in the process of not holding their alcohol—but the wildlife rarely knows what they are talking about.

Famous American Indians Whom You May Not Have Known Were American Indians
- Cher
- Elvis Presley
- Scottie Pippen
- Johnny Depp
- Cameron Diaz

Famous American Indians Who Actually Are Not American Indians
- Everyone from *F Troop*
- The Indian from the Village People

Indians

When we say *Indians* or *East Indians,* we are referring to descendants of the nation of India, and all of the surrounding "Indian-y" countries and islands. Many consider the Indians to be the funniest of ethnic groups in North America. Maybe it's their accent, maybe it's their food . . . maybe it's the thing with the cows. But while everyone is laughing at them, they are slowly but surely taking over the fields of technology, engineering, and medicine. They are also cornering the market in funny Indian convenience-store clerks on animated TV shows (or are they?).

Ever since the partitioning of India in 1947, there has been a long-simmering conflict between Indians and Pakistanis, which can also be seen between Indian-Americans and Pakistani-

Americans. For the record, here is a helpful diagram to distinguish between the two vastly different groups.

Compare and Contrast: Indians and Pakistanis

The Similarities between Indians and Pakistanis
- Highly educated
- Family-oriented
- Hardworking
- Deeply spiritual

The Differences
- Pakistanis are slightly worse at driving a taxi

Names

The most unusual characteristic of Indian names is that they are all impossible to spell. This may explain why Indian kids always win that big spelling bee on TV every year.

Occupations

• Doctors

Thousands of Indian doctors are working in hospitals across the country. Almost all of them are stuck working in emergency rooms. They rarely move beyond that post due to their poor communication skills and lack of interest in golf.

• Convenience-Store Owners

Unable to scale the highest heights of the medical field, Indians have been able to dominate the convenience-store business due to their poor communication skills and lack of interest in golf.

• Restaurateurs

Indians pride themselves on the complexity and spiciness of their cuisine. But upon further investigation, it turns out that the only reason the food is so spicy is to cover up the taste of rancid goat meat and week-old okra.

Ironically, the only food that Indian food is actually better than is Indian food (the other Indians—you know, maize and bear grease).

Enemies

Indians have many enemies due to long-standing rivalries between Indians and Pakistanis, Hindus and Muslims, and 7-Eleven and Cumberland Market.

Misconceptions and Stereotypes

• Their music is bad

It is a cruel and dangerous stereotype to say that Indian music is bad. Indian music is atrocious. Just calling it bad does a disservice to actual bad musicians such as Billy Joel.

• They don't eat beef

Many Indians do not eat beef. Some Indians do eat beef. All Indians wish they ate beef.

Famous Indians Who Actually Aren't Indian

- Apu (store manager from *The Simpsons* is actually Greek-American Hank Azaria)

Famous Indians You Didn't Know Were Indian

- Norah Jones (Ravi Shankar's daughter)
- Chipper Jones (Ravi Shankar's son—paternity test pending)

Famous Indians Who Actually Are Indian

- Sanjay Gupta (doctor/reporter)
- Bobby Jindal (governor of Louisiana)
- Ravi Shankar (father)

Latino/Hispanic

A long-standing debate concerns the comparative meanings of *Latino* and *Hispanic*. Both terms can be used to describe people whose origins can be traced to Spanish-speaking countries. Ironically, most Americans living abroad will soon be able to call themselves Latino (or Hispanic) since pretty much everyone here speaks Spanish now.

A recent poll conducted by the Hispanic Heritage Plaza of twelve hundred registered Latino voters (which, ironically, is the total number of all registered Latino voters in the United States) showed 65 percent preferred the term *Hispanic* and 30 percent preferred the term *Latino*.

The remaining 5 percent preferred to be called:

1.8% Kinda Mexican-ish
1.1% The Taco Bell Dog
.9%   The Whole Enchilada
.6%   Some Guys Named Jose
.4%   Natives of the Lost Island of Atlantis
.2%   Dwight David Eisenhower

Whatever they want to be called, we will be using *Hispanic* and *Latino* interchangeably to analyze the largest non-White ethnic group in the United States.

Latinos are everywhere. They have spread across every corner of this nation. Since they reproduce faster than Starbucks franchises, it is expected that they will soon be the single largest ethnic group in the United States. However, before you go running out to your nearest mall to purchase an English-Spanish dictionary, you should know that most Latinos speak less Spanish than Nicole Ritchie.

Many ethnic researchers are tempted to lump all Hispanics into one statistical clump, as if they were a big burrito filled with Mexicans, Puerto Ricans, Pico de Gallo, Dominicans, and Sour Cream. The Hechinger Method, however, has conclusively proven that substantial differences exist between the wide variety of Hispanic subspecies. Nonetheless, we have observed certain generalities:

Family Size

All Hispanics have huge families—unless they are impotent, infertile, or gay. Frankly, even some impotent, infertile, and gay Hispanic couples have managed to have seventeen children. Within these enormous families, many generations live together under one roof—although sometimes there isn't a roof at all. They respect their elders and are famous for taking excellent care of the oldest members of their families, who always live with them. However, as Hispanic household incomes increase, it is anticipated that they will stick the geezers into nursing homes like all the other rich people do.

Transportation
- Pickup trucks
- Burros
- Lowrider cars
- The insides of emptied gas tankers
- Lexus convertibles (George Lopez)

Accessories
- Hair products that smell like tropical fruit
- Car fresheners that smell like tropical fruit
- Tropical fruit

Aphrodisiacs

Latinos spurn the use of aphrodisiacs. According to California governor (and erstwhile movie celebrity) Arnold Schwarzenegger, this is because they are "hot-blooded." Of course, Mr. Schwarzenegger also thinks that Blacks "can't swim" and that women "all want it."

Physical Characteristics

Despite a wide range of physical characteristics within the Hispanic community, certain patterns can be noted. Hispanics tend to be short, brownish, and squat, with broad noses and dark hair. Like little brown bears who love tacos and stealing hubcaps.

Geography

As mentioned earlier, Latinos are the fastest-growing ethnic group in North America. This can be attributed to the cultural approval of large families, religious restrictions on contraception, and the astounding degree to which tequila makes one lose one's inhibitions while still maintaining an erection.

Originally, Latinos were concentrated in areas of warm weather. Let's face it, February in Chicago isn't exactly Sunday at the beach in Oaxaca. But recent improvements in down-coat technology have led to the dispersal of Latinos across the country.

Natural Predators

- Unscrupulous Border Patrol agents
- Unscrupulous Immigration agents
- Unscrupulous Major League Baseball agents

Common Names

For males: Juan, Carlos, Miguel. That's it. Anyone claiming to be Hispanic whose name isn't Juan, Carlos, or Miguel is a liar.

For females: Gloria, Maria—pretty much anything ending in *ia* except for *malaria*. In Houston, Texas, we met a charming young lady named Diphtheria Garcia.

By the way, Garcia has now become one of the top ten most common surnames in the United States. Surprisingly, the most popular first name in Mexico is Dave.

Latino Subspecies

Cuban-Americans

Cuban-Americans don't consider themselves American so much as they consider themselves exiles from the closest thing to paradise on Earth: pre-Castro Cuba. The rest of the country is willing to put up with their condescension, however, because the actual closest thing to paradise on Earth is a freshly pressed Cuban sandwich. And let's face it, without Cuban-Americans, there'd be no Cuban sandwiches here.

Cubans are a proud people who have strongly held beliefs, such as:

- Refrigerators are seaworthy vessels
- It's okay to wear a tropical shirt with a forest of chest hair showing to any occasion (including meeting the Pope)
- Overthrowing Castro will result in the return of a vibrant democracy just like the one Cubans had back when Cuba was a puppet of the American government and the Mafia

═ LITTLE-KNOWN FACT ═

The Cuban-American Assault on Cuba

A few months after the Cuban Missile Crisis, a group of exiled Cuban-Americans living in Miami attempted an audacious attack on Cuba in hopes of overthrowing the Castro regime.

Their effort was led by Juan Florez, who assembled an entire armada out of high-quality cardboard refrigerator boxes. His goal was an early-morning surprise attack across the ninety miles between the two countries. Unfortunately, the assault was cut short as the boats were immediately swamped with water and sank. All the brave patriots died, but the cardboard, thank God, was saved and recycled. To this day, you can own a piece of history if you have a pizza delivered in Miami.

Famous Cuban-Americans
- Captain Morgan
- Desi Arnaz
- The following Major League Baseball players:

CUBAN-AMERICAN MAJOR LEAGUE BASEBALL PLAYERS CHART

Jose Acosta
Merito Acosta
Rafael Almeida
Luis Aloma
Ossie Alvarez
Rogelio Alvarez
Vicente Amor
Sandy Amoros
Angel Aragon
Jack Aragon
Jose Arcia
Rudy Arias
Rene Arocha
Rolando Arrojo
Joe Azcue
Danys Baez
Ed Bauta
Julio Becquer
Yuniesky Betancourt
Jack Calvo
Bert Campaneris
Frank Campos
Jose Canseco
Ozzie Canseco
Jose Cardenal
Leo Cardenas
Paul Casanova
Jorge Comellas
Sandy Consuegra
Jose Contreras
Mike Cuellar
Bert Cueto
Manuel Cueto
Juan Delis
Orestes Destrade
Juan Diaz
Pedro Dibut
Lino Donoso

Yunel Escobar
Bobby Estalella
Oscar Estrada
Chico Fernandez
Osvaldo Fernandez
Angel Fleitas
Mike Fornieles
Tony Fossas
Tito Fuentes
Barbaro Garbey
Ramon Garcia
Preston Gomez
Vince Gonzales
Eusebio Gonzalez
Julio Gonzalez
Mike Gonzalez
Orlando Gonzalez
Tony Gonzalez
Mike Guerra
Adrian Hernandez
Chico Hernandez
Evelio Hernandez
Jackie Hernandez
Livan Hernandez
Michel Hernandez
Orlando Hernandez
Mike Herrera
Pancho Herrera
Hank Izquierdo
Hansel Izquierdo
George Lauzerique
Izzy Leon
Marcelino Lopez
Ramon Lopez
Dolf Luque
Hector Maestri
Connie Marrero
Eli Marrero

Armando Marsans
Hector Martinez
Jose Martinez
Marty Martinez
Rogelio Martinez
Tony Martinez
Orlando McFarlane
Roman Mejias
Minnie Mendoza
Tony Menendez
Minnie Minoso
Willy Miranda
Aurelio Monteagudo
Rene Monteagudo
Manny Montejo
Kendry Morales
Danny Morejon
Julio Moreno
Cholly Naranjo
Ray Noble
Vladimir Nunez
Tony Oliva
Tony Ordenana
Rey Ordonez
Eddie Oropesa
Bill Ortega
Baby Ortiz
Roberto Ortiz
Reggie Otero
Rafael Palmeiro
Emilio Palmero
Camilo Pascual
Carlos Pascual
Carlos Paula
Brayan Pena
Orlando Pena
Tony Perez
Leo Posada

Ariel Prieto
Bobby Ramos
Pedro Ramos
Nap Reyes
Armando Roche
Freddy Rodriguez
Hector Rodriguez
Jose Rodriguez
Cookie Rojas
Minnie Rojas
Chico Ruiz
Alex Sanchez
Israel Sanchez
Raul Sanchez
Nelson Santovenia
Diego Segui
Alay Soler
Luis Suarez
Leo Sutherland
Jose Tartabull
Tony Taylor
Michael Tejera
Luis Tiant
Jorge Toca
Gil Torres
Ricardo Torres
Sandy Ullrich
Roy Valdes
Sandy Valdespino
Rene Valdez
Jose Valdivielso
Zoilo Versalles
Adrian Zabala
Oscar Zamora
Jose Zardon
Tommy de la Cruz
Mike de la Hoz

(And these are just the Cubans from Santiago)

Education and Income
According to the Jens Jenning Census of 2007, Cuban-Americans tend to graduate from college at a higher rate and make more money than most other Hispanic subgroups. They also tend to blow most of their money at the dog races.

Puerto Ricans

The "original" Latino immigrants, Puerto Ricans, first settled in the greater New York metropolis, which remains their primary nesting area.

The history of Puerto Rico and Puerto Ricans is one of sifting and shifting ethnicities (White, Brown, Black, and Yellow). Not surprisingly, this racial mixture has, at times, led to a sense of confusion and the desire to make Puerto Rico the fifty-first state. Over the years, the island of Puerto Rico has been a stopping-off place for pirates, privateers, slaves, slave owners, and wealthy Jews trying to keep themselves occupied during Christmas vacation.

The Jewish-American Princess versus the Puerto Rican–American Princess (JAP vs. PRAP)

The seminal Loche Study (Brookings Institution, March 2008) revealed the single most telling difference between these two groups: PRAPs wear fake jewelry and have real orgasms. JAPs wear real jewelry and fake orgasms. Everything else is the same.

JEWISH-AMERICAN PRINCESS   PUERTO RICAN–AMERICAN PRINCESS

Real Jewelry
Fake Orgasms

Fake Jewelry
Real Orgasms

BONUS SECTION

The *Ch* Predictor Factor

One interesting by-product of our analysis of Puerto Rican culture was the *ch* predictor of consumption. We found that a significant proportion of bestselling consumer products begin with the *ch* sound.

- The most popular car: Chevy
- The most popular Scotch: Chivas
- The most popular soccer team: Chivas
- The most popular gum: Chiclets
- The most popular beer: Tecate (But *Sch*aefer was a close second)

Dominican-Americans

Referred to as Domes or Dumbinicans by those foolhardy enough to make up silly nicknames for any ethnic group, this subspecies initially settled in an area near the George Washington Bridge in Manhattan. We surmise that this choice of locale was because Dominicans traditionally love baseball and they wanted to be near America's shrine to the game, the Cloisters.

Dominicans are hardworking, love sugary pastries, and produce superlative baseball players, including Juan Marichal, César Cedeño, and hundreds and hundreds of Alou brothers including Jesús, Matty, Felipe, Harpo, Banana Hammock, Murray, and David. Moisés Alou is Felipe Alou's son but has always considered his real father to be Banana Hammock Alou.

TWO LITTLE-KNOWN FACTS

1. Dominican-Americans are the hairdressers of choice for Blacks in New York City. So, if you think that P. Diddy's 'fro looks lame, complain to a Dominican.

2. Many people from the Dominican Republic left their homeland *not* because they wanted to leave, but because they freaked out when they discovered they were sharing an island with Haiti.

Mexican-Americans

MAs are, in sheer numbers, the big "enchilada" of the Latino/ Hispanic ethnic group. Recent estimates have established that, by the year 2070, the entire population of Mexico will be living in the United States. Due to tax problems and outsourced industrial jobs, however, the entire population of the United States will be living in Mexico by then—so things ought to work out just fine.

Nesting Habits

Mexican-Americans have proven to be extremely adaptable. They live in cities, they live on farms, they live in the backs of flatbed trucks.

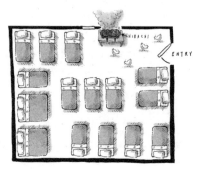

TYPICAL HABITAT OF THE NOT-SO
AFFLUENT NORTH AMERICAN
HISPANICS AND LATINOS
(LEGAL OR OTHERWISE)

Famous Mexican-Americans
- Jessica Alba
- There are lots more, but who's gonna top Jessica Alba?

Famous Mexican-Americans Who Aren't Actually Mexican-Americans
- Taco Bell Chihuahua (Carlos Alazraqui is actually of Argentine extraction)
- Speedy Gonzalez (Mel Blanc was a Jew from San Francisco)
- Frito Bandito (see Mel Blanc)
- Alberto Gonzales (surprisingly, also a Jew from San Francisco)

Mexican-American Sports
- Soccer
- Street drag racing
- How many people can a Toyota hold?
- Hide-and-seek (frequently from immigration officers)

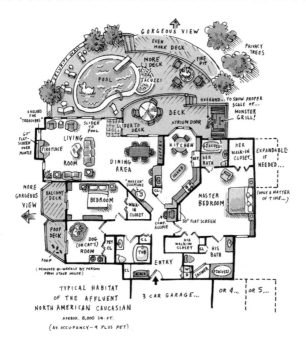

TYPICAL HABITAT
OF THE AFFLUENT
NORTH AMERICAN CAUCASIAN
APPROX. 8,000 SQ. FT.
(AV. OCCUPANCY—4 PLUS PET)

Migratory Patterns

Mexican-Americans move around. Most of this migratory movement is in search of harvesting jobs, but sometimes it's just so they can find a better spot near the freeway from which to sell you oranges.

Why Does Everyone Pick on the Mexicans?

After Blacks and Jews, Mexicans would appear to be the ethnic group most often chosen as the butt of silly, usually offensive jokes. We conducted a blind interview session to attempt to discover why this is so. Unfortunately, the blind people whom we interviewed had no opinions on this subject. They did have uncannily excellent senses of smell, however.

In Defense of the Mexicans

Not that they need defending, but we feel obligated to point out some really impressive qualities of the Mexican-American that we discovered during our years of extensive research, watching them mow our lawns. By and large, Mexican-Americans are:

- Good problem solvers
- Family-oriented
- Deeply religious
- Natural carpoolers
- Supremely gifted at "taking it easy"

Guatemalan-Americans

GAs are a small group (both numbers-wise and in terms of stature) who are making their presence felt more and more in the United States. They have made serious inroads in the fields of stone masonry, furniture restoration, and child care. So, if you need your six-year-old watched by someone who can cut marble and distress mahogany, call a Guatemalan.

Colombian/Peruvian-Americans

While they hail from two vastly different countries (note the variations between *patasca* and *mondongo*), Colombian-Americans and Peruvian-Americans have a great deal in common. Relatively recent additions to this country's ethnic makeup, they have both achieved great success in the housepainting business. Much like brush-wielding acrobats or agile monkeys jabbering in Spanish, a dozen Colombian- or Peruvian-Americans can paint even the most enormous home in a day.

C/PAs are also supremely talented at owning and operating delicious and inexpensive eateries on the outskirts of most major

American cities. Just stay out of them during World Cup soccer games (unless you're sure that Colombia and Peru are going to win).

Arab/Middle Eastern Americans

Americans whose ancestry can be traced to the Middle East, and we're including such countries as Lebanon, Syria, Iraq, Egypt, and Iran, are perhaps the least understood of all ethnic groups living in this country. So we thought we'd try to set the record straight. Before we start, however, we want to make one thing clear: we have tremendous respect for all these people, and we really don't want anyone to put a fatwa out on us. Thanks in advance.

Here are some interesting and fun facts about Middle Eastern Americans:

- Most Arabs are not Muslims
- Most Muslims are not Arabs
- All Arabs are Arabs
- Some Muslims are Jewish
- Not all Muslims are terrorists
- Not all terrorists are Muslims, or Arabs
- Only Black Muslims wear those little bow ties
- Danny Thomas did not have a woman defecate on a glass table while he was underneath it (he was sitting in a chair)

Geographical Distribution

Nearly 40 percent of Arab-Americans live in New York, Detroit, and Los Angeles. Another 5 percent are on vacation in the Caribbean (Guantánamo Bay). And 2 percent are stuck in those special screening rooms at the airport and will never make it to their cousin's in Atlanta in time for the Super Bowl.

As for Muslims of Iranian or Syrian descent, we couldn't find any at all. We heard that there were a bunch near a nuclear power plant in Pennsylvania, but someone shot at us as we drove up and we took off.

Jobs/Occupations

Hardworking, family-oriented, and real sticklers on female chastity, Middle Eastern Americans are prevalent in sales, medicine, and any other sector where haggling over prices is an effective negotiating tactic. Some of the other occupations at which Middle Eastern Americans have been successful are:

- Pistachio, date, and fig growing
- The rug trade—carpets, that is (the Greeks dominate the toupee business)
- Playing bad guys in movies

Here's another reason the Indians have to be pissed off at the White man. For years, the bad guys were always the Indians. But over the past fifteen years (and especially since 9/11) the default bad guy is automatically some swarthy dude with a desert accent and a head scarf. Oh well, at least they haven't opened any Muslim casinos here yet.

Famous Arab-Americans
- Paula Abdul
- Jamie Farr
- Tony Shalhoub
- Casey Kasem
- Doug Flutie
- Tiny Tim

Rumor has it that Tiny Tim actually trained Doug Flutie in his unorthodox throwing style since it is common knowledge that Flutie was rather "tiny" himself. (In the spirit of full disclosure, please note that these rumors were started by us. Just now.)

Muslim-American Religious Extremists

MAREs are an interesting immigrant ethnic group. Much like the earliest European arrivals to this land, they have also come here for religious freedom. Unfortunately, their idea of religious freedom is to destroy our financial infrastructure, kill us all, and then bang virgins forever in the afterlife.

The actual number of MAREs currently living in the United States varies greatly depending on whom you ask. According to the FBI, there are seven. According to the overwhelming neuroses that liquefy our bowels and keep us awake at night, there are five-hundred thousand. The truth is probably somewhere in between.

Jobs/Vocations
- Pilots
- Nuclear power plant operators
- Flammable-explosive tank-truck drivers
- Gold Club members at Hooters

ETHNIC DEMOGRAPHIC

CHAPTER IV

WHITES

According to the dictionary, the definition of White as an ethnicity is "a member of a race that is characterized by pale skin, i.e., light pigmentation of the skin." In other words, White people. So, now that we have explained our dense, scientific terminology, let's get on with it.

Biological Precedent

Although some believe that Adam and Eve looked as if they walked out of a Ralph Lauren ad, common scientific theory holds that human life began either somewhere in the Middle East or somewhere in Africa. Whichever way you go, you have to figure that White people didn't start squat.

As humans moved farther away to more temperate climes, they lost their pigment, as it was not needed to protect them against the harsh sun. This also explains why Latvian men still have a blanket of hair on their back, but doesn't necessarily explain why Swedish women have pleasantly perky bosoms.

Another theory, put forth by noted anthropologist and ex-harness-jockey Eugene Colatrava, suggests that ancient aboriginal tribes with lighter skin pigmentation flourished because they could play dead better and were more adept at finding good hiding places, thus avoiding bloodthirsty invaders.

Whatever their history, Whites have dominated the ethnic scene in this country ever since they arrived. Their first successful move was to wipe out all of the indigenous people by shooting a lot of them and infecting the rest with smallpox. Whites in America are the New York Yankees of ethnic groups—they have a long tradition of "winning," although the Yankees will never be forgiven for blowing that 3–0 lead in the 2004 ALCS.

Much like the Yankees, however, Whites have many detractors. A lot of these critics believe that Whites are innately inferior due to the thing that makes them White—their very lack of color.

"In my view, it is the 'white race' that is lacking . . . they lack melanin (pigment) and thus are MISSING something the 'darker races' have. They also have a distinct lack of rhythm and they believe that they look good in madras shorts, which is obviously a genetic disorder. I don't care what Abercrombie & Fitch™ says, those shorts should all be collected and burned in an extremely colorful bonfire that would probably smell like sunscreen and cheap cologne" (Dr. Norman Buckles, *The Long and Short of Shorts* [St. Martin's Press, 2002]).

If you consider Spaniards and Italians to be Whites (and only they do), then Whites started coming to America in the fifteenth century. Most early White immigrants came for economic opportunity and religious freedom. But these people were pretty much the dregs of European society and were hated by everyone else. Given the option, they would probably have gone to Newark in August rather than stay where they were. Of course, technically, some of them did go to Newark in August. The Europeans they left behind were eager to see them leave. So were many of the European farm animals. The queen paid their way, for God's sake. These are the kinds of White people who built this great land.

How We Organized This Chapter

Rather than operate on a nationality-based ethnic scale, we have organized the White chapter slightly differently: we have employed the patented Hechinger Sliding Color Scale. Our uncle Fritz generated this complex computer program from the computer room of the minimum-security facility in which he'll be spending the next thirty-six to sixty months. The HSCS analyzes all ethnic groups and distills them into an average color hue. So, we fed all the different kinds of Whites into the supercomputer, flipped the HSCS on, and it came up with the following sequencing. At one end of the White Scale is White White. Then it descends into a variety of increasingly less White hues including Off-White, Ecru, Eggshell, Dusk, Nearly White, and finally, Not Particularly White at All. Look for these color shadings in our new Hechinger home paint fall collection.

1. Albinos

You can argue until you're blue in the face, but White folks just don't come any Whiter than Albinos. The lack of melanin in their skin causes their driven-snow pigmentation. It is a hereditary condition, although some studies suggest exposure to heavy metals can cause this change. This seems unlikely, as our cousin Barry listens to nothing but Metallica and Iron Maiden, and he's actually on the swarthy side.

Since Albinos are only a tiny minority of the White community, we're not going to spend much time with them. They are a simple, God-fearing people who, over the centuries, have often been misunderstood. If we had a nickel for every time someone persecuted

Albinos for being witches or for having perceived mind-reading abilities, why—we'd have almost a dollar.

Geographically speaking, they have no clearly defined areas of concentration. They tend to avoid climates with extended, searing sunshine, because if Albinos spend too much time outdoors, they will burst into flames. It's a little-known fact, but irresponsible Albinos hiking with their shirts off are the cause of 64 percent of the country's forest fires.

Although they are occasionally perceived as "weird," "spooky," or "witchlike," Albinos are not perceptibly different from everyone else—except for their skin tone . . . and for the fact that some of them are weird, spooky witches.

Because pigment is essential for the development of the cornea, they do tend to have visual issues. This is why you rarely see Albino airline pilots. And if you do, you might want to think about rescheduling your flight.

Common Misperceptions about Albinos
- They can read your mind
- They are see-through
- They glow purple in black light
- They go as themselves for Halloween

Famous Albinos
- Johnny and Edgar Winter (blues rock guitarists)
- Wow, there really aren't a lot of Albinos, are there?

2. Scandinavian-Americans
For reasons of clarity (and because these are an inordinately boring people), we've grouped the Danes, Finns, Swedes, and Norwegians into one group, whom we'll call Scandi-Americans. When

Scandis first came to this country, they settled mainly in the upper Midwest because it was cold and they could be near cows, cheese, and the Packers—all of which they adore.

Physical Attributes

Once tall, fair-skinned, fair-haired, and handsome, the Scandi-Americans' gift for assimilation has created a shorter, stouter species that lacks the bold, sensual quality of their genetic ancestors.

Many Scandi-Americans in the Great Lakes region have spent so much time consuming dairy products, eating baked goods, and sitting out the snows on their living room sofas, they have fundamentally altered their genetic code. Their women used to be stunning beauties. Now they all look like Danny DeVito.

Nesting Patterns

Scandi-Americans predominantly settled in the upper Midwest but have become quite dispersed geographically. We hear rumors that some Scandi-Americans are even living in South Dakota, but we couldn't corroborate that information because we accidentally drove right through South Dakota without noticing.

To specifically identify this highly assimilated group, we created the ABBA Test™. We approached subjects and asked them if they could name a song by the Swedish pop band ABBA. If they could, then they were Scandi-Americans. If they knew the name of a song and all of the lyrics, then they were gay Scandi-Americans.

SAs are masters of all things dairy. In fact, in some circles they are referred to as lactose savants. Of course, those are very strange circles. Famous transplanted Swedish actor Peter Stormare has gone on record saying that if he has a child, he will name that child—boy or girl—Butter Milk Stormare. Fortunately for us all, Mr. Stormare's wife wisely gave him a home vasectomy while he slept off a wicked Absolut hangover.

Myth Buster

A common misperception among some is that the dog breed Great Danes descended from actual Danish people. We can officially and permanently debunk this erroneous assumption. The Great Dane actually descended from the Swedish people. They had frequent relations with a native dog breed, and when the dogs actually got pregnant, they were horrified that the world would find out what they'd done. So, they named the puppies Great Danes and fled for Norway.

How to Spot a Scandi-American
Because they meld so well into the fabric of average American life, SAs can be difficult to identify. Here are some subtle behaviors that can tip you off to the presence of a Scandi-American:

- They hold hands and dance around a Christmas tree
- They can talk for hours about dairy farming
- They know who Jacob Riis was
- They admit they like herring and not just for the omega-3
- They smell like lingonberries

Other Things You Should Know

The Finns are sometimes referred to as the dumbest of the Scandinavians. Witness this joke:

Q: Why don't the Finns fish in winter?

A: Because they can't cut a hole big enough for their boat.

Ha! That's stupid. See, Swedes, Danes, and Norwegians are so smart that when they want to fish in winter, they cut a little hole in the ice and they sit on their butts for hours, freezing in the snow and sleet until they catch an eight-inch pike that's inedible. Brilliant!

Finns make the best bartenders due to their love of alcohol, ice, and listening to other drunk people complain about the lackluster herring catch.

Nearly a third of the population of Montana claims Norwegian ancestry. So, there's sixteen Norwegian-Americans right there.

Scandi-American Contributions to Society
- Licorice
- Swedish fish
- Swedish massage
- Swedish meatballs
- IKEA

Scandi-American Blights on Society
- Dane Cook

Scandi-American Subspecies

• Upper-Midwest Middle-Class Nordics

UMMCNs highly value family structure and traditions. Males love ice fishing, and women love trying to find new ways of mixing potatoes and cheese. Their default philosophical position is that people are inherently "good." Of course, they also think that obese people can wear skinny jeans, so you just can't trust them.

• Upper East Side Swedish Executive

This man is a walking Scandinavian cliché. He drives a SAAB, he wears clogs, he eats salt cod and drinks aquavit. The only problem is that he doesn't speak a word of any Scandinavian language and, when he goes on vacation, refuses to travel north of South Beach, Florida.

• The Scandi Poker Player

An increasingly common sight at the felt tables of Las Vegas, Reno, and Uncasville, Connecticut, the SPP prides himself (and it's always a man for some reason) on having blood as cold as his homeland's winters. He is usually hairless and wears his shirts open to his navel. SPPs have been extremely successful at winning fortunes at high-stakes poker tables around the world. If you come up against one, immediately fold your hand and walk away. Unless you are a Vietnamese Poker Player, in which case you should move all-in, get lucky, and win the big one.

3. English-Americans

The English were the first to migrate to this continent in large numbers. Once proud and dominant, the inheritors of the British legacy have been bowed by decreased expectations, a shoddy work ethic, and a woefully underachieving national soccer team.

ENDANGERED SPECIES ALERT! THE WASP

Where once WASPs were America's burgeoning superrace, they are now relegated to gleaning a vestige of their erstwhile pride by checking "non-Hispanic" on government forms. For the first few hundred years after they arrived from Britain, WASPs dominated all facets of North American society.

For the sake of clarity, let us once again define our terms. Technically speaking, a WASP is a White Anglo-Saxon Protestant. Although, in practical terms, a WASP is really anyone who gets out of the shower to take a leak.

If you want to learn more about WASPs but you're sick of reading, make sure to rent HBO's excellent miniseries *John Adams,* which effectively portrays the dominance of the Englishman in America. Obviously, the story took place before all the WASPs started playing golf, but you'll still get the idea. The mighty WASPs, who were the result of the metaphorical marriage between Great Britain and the New World, dominated the spheres of business, politics, religion, and education for centuries. It should come as no surprise, then, that our current businesses, politics, religions, and educational systems are so completely screwed up.

The Tipping Point

At what precise moment did the hegemony of the WASP end? Was it in 1980 with the publication of *The Official Preppy Handbook*? Or was it, as some say, May 25, 1985, when Michael Jackson electrified a worldwide audience at the Motown anniversary show by moonwalking? That one series of tiny steps for man proved to be a gigantic leap in proving once and for all that WASPs—no matter how much education at Harvard or money on Wall Street—were never going to be able to rule again. They would also never be able to moonwalk.

But our sophisticated pie charts designed to calculate the shifts in cultural zeitgeist to a margin of error less than one-eighth of pi point to a different moment when the WASP bit the dust. We humbly suggest that the beginning of the end for WASP predominance in North America can be traced to Dan Quayle, the unctuous, overachieving scion of a small-town Midwestern family. It was obvious to millions that even though a retarded toddler left in a Dumpster to eat paint chips had a keener intellect than him, Dan Quayle was destined for greatness.

After all, this is the man who uttered these unforgettable words:

"It is time for the human race to enter the solar system."

Okay, so we've got a rich, stupid, well-connected WASP who is great at golf . . . What's next? The vice presidency! Everything was on track when the strangest thing happened. Everyone suddenly realized that Dan Quayle was a moron . . . *and they resented it!*

This was the first time that a WASP male was actually stopped from coasting his way to the presidency. People woke up to the reality that maybe—just maybe—being a child of ethnic privilege wasn't a sufficient enough criterion to rule the world.

Obviously, the people didn't learn their lesson very well, since they went on to elect George W. Bush twice—but the seeds were sown. WASPs may still be on the top rung of society's ladder, but their grip is starting to slip.

By 2070, we estimate there will be fewer than five hundred WASPs left in the United States. Relegated to cultural oddities and tourist attractions, most of them will probably operate roadside shacks near Hilton Head, South Carolina, where they will sell boat shoes and homemade argyle sweater vests to a passing swarm of affluent Gullahs and Geechees heading to the links to play golf.

4. Land-Rich, Cash-Poor Southerners

This group is very White, but not quite as White as they used to be. They're highly educated—both academically and socially. They know all about the Council of Trent and which fork is supposed to be used to eat cucumbers. They speak in charming, lilting accents and make rum drinks invented by their great-great-grandfathers, who were the kinds of Civil War generals who never did anything mean to Black people. They publish books of poetry and create original rose hybrids all the time. They have beautiful mansions in Charlotte and Savannah and Roanoke. Their only problem is that they've squandered every penny their ancestors ever made in their relentless pursuit of poetry classes and horticultural lectures. So, now they all work at Burger King.

5. The Greenwich Hedge-Fund Manager

Just a hair down the White scale from these genteel Southerners are the Greenwich, Connecticut, Hedge-Fund Managers. For the most part this group is exceedingly WASPy and reserved. They take great pride in keeping any semblance of actual personality in check—unless they get drunk after work at Hooters, in which case they reveal their personalities, which tend to be boorish and loathsome.

GHFMs can be spotted driving through Fairfield County in six-hundred-horsepower, fire-breathing Maseratis . . . at two miles an hour. They do this to make sure that everyone knows how fast a car they have. See, if they drove it fast, then no one would know it was them driving. They're a complicated people.

As White as they are, the only reason that they are lower down on the White scale is that one has to factor into this ethnic group the occasional Indian or Asian Greenwich Hedge-Fund Manager. While these folks do tend to darken the pot, no one resents them because they're the ones who figure out all the new ways to turn millions into billions.

6. German-Americans

A little-known fact is that more people claim German heritage in America than any other ethnicity. Of course, Mexicans will surpass that number in another week or so.

Geographical Distribution

Germans settled mainly in the Midwest and West, although Pennsylvania and upstate New York have significant populations. Prior to World War II they boasted of their Germanic bloodlines. Since then, many have decided to play their "Deutsch cards" closer to the vest. Fortunately for German-Americans, the past sixty years have seen us engage in so many fierce battles with so many different countries that pretty much no one remembers that the Germans used to be our enemies. Heinz and Adolph are becoming more and more popular names for kids who will inevitably get beaten up at school.

Much of the Midwest was originally settled by German-

Americans—after they chased off the Indians. And, of course, by "chased off" we mean "murdered." St. Louis, Cincinnati, and Milwaukee form what is still called the German Triangle.

Always gifted mathematicians, German-Americans also boast the "German Parallelogram," which stretches across a great swath of the upper half of our country.

For the record, neither the German Triangle nor the German Parallelogram should be confused with the Russian Rhombus, the Transylvanian Trapezoid, or the Syrian Circle (which, thankfully, is no longer active due to recent FBI intervention).

Famous German-Americans
- Babe Ruth
- Marlene Dietrich
- Dwight Eisenhower
- Fred Astaire
- William Boeing
- Eberhard Anheuser
- Walter Chrysler
- The Donner Party
- Clark Gable
- Henry Heinz
- Milton Hershey

Not So Famous German-Americans
- Martin Herbst
- Billy Spaetzel
- Heinrich "Boom Boom" Manheim

German-American subspecies

First of all, a complex and confusing argument concerns whether different religions factor into different ethnicities. Are Irish Catholics ethnically different from Irish Protestants? Are German-American Jews less White than German-American Mormons? Why don't Hindus eat beef? The bottom line is, we don't care. We will arbitrarily choose when we ethnically differentiate between religions and when we just decide to lump everyone in together.

That said, when it comes to identifying German-Americans in a crowd, they can be very hard to pick out, since they have become so assimilated into our national culture. It would be much easier if they all went around wearing brown shirts and goose-stepping, but that hardly ever happens outside Idaho.

Dr. Aaron Klinkenstein found in his groundbreaking study in 2004 that if you whispered the word *sauerkraut,* most people of German ancestry would give you a slight nod followed by a subtle grin. But this technique is iffy at best and downright embarrassing at worst. So, for ease of identification, we have divided German-Americans into some more recognizable subsets.

A. Overeducated, Condescending German Jews

A significant number of German Jews came to America in the early part of the century when they realized that their options were to either take a long, unpleasant sea voyage or die. Many of these folks were highly educated. The fact that they suddenly found themselves in a country where most people thought that Mozart was the name of a painting-supply store probably led to their generally condescending attitude. Also, a lot of them wore thin wire glasses that were too small for their faces, which can't help but make you look condescending.

The OCGJs have been successful in the fields of academia, Wall

Street, real estate, show business, and hair removal. To honor the motherland that tried to eradicate them, they buy German luxury cars by the boatload.

B. Dutch Country Quakers

Surprisingly, Dutch Country Quakers are neither Dutch nor do they necessarily live in the country. They are, however, Quakers. A sect of predominantly German-Americans residing mainly in southeastern Pennsylvania, they stress strict adherence to religious law and plainness in speech and appearance. This plainness is quite evident if you've ever come across a Quaker chick. They are a simple people who like to live among themselves. They eschew technology and modern culture, though they love the new Lil Wayne album.

C. The Amish

Contrary to what you may have learned in the movie *Witness,* Amish people are not all superattractive and dying to have sex with strangers. Most of them just want to be left alone to churn their butter and build their houses by hand in a day.

We discovered a surprising link between the Amish and the Orthodox Jewish Hasidim. It is unlikely that an Amish person and a Hasid have ever had sex with each other. Frankly, it's a miracle that an Amish person or a Hasid have ever had sex with anyone. But at some point the groups came across one another, checked out the other's look, and said, "Wow, that's a snazzy getup. From now on we're gonna wear nothing but all-black outfits, occasionally dusted with dandruff."

Similar to the Quakers and the Amish, the Shakers are also of German descent.

You're hosting a barbecue. One of two strange men dressed all in black ordered a plate of baby back ribs, but you don't know which man. One of them will say "Thankee kindly," while the other will run away shouting "Oy gevalt!" Knowing the difference between an Amish man and a Hasidic Jew could be the key to making your barbecue sink or swim! Here's how to do it: The Hasid is on the right. You can tell because that slight bulge in his jacket pocket is the deed to the Amish man's house.

D. The Shakers

No, these are not the people who lie on the floor in church and wiggle like eels because the spirit of the Lord has entered them. Those people are called epileptics. And *Shakers* is also not the name of a group of large-breasted women in Las Vegas who shake their bodies in exchange for cash. Those people are called Women in Las Vegas. Shakers are a small group of German-Americans whose fierce belief in chastity basically made them extinct. Fortunately, they made some very nice furniture before they all died, which is worth a lot of money now.

E. Former Nazi Commanders in Hiding

This group is a surprisingly large but hard-to-prove-that-they-exist subsegment consisting of old men living boring middle-class lives, mostly in sleepy, suburban culs-de-sac.

By all accounts they are normal neighbors, with typical wives and children and jobs. Basically they're just like the rest of us—except that they all have secret rooms in their basements where they regularly reenact the Anschluss while making loud explosive noises with their mouths.

If you watch them carefully though, they cannot walk more than twenty yards without reflexively goose-stepping. If they spot you watching, they will immediately catch themselves, return to a normal gait, and ask how your Little League game went.

F. Midwestern Cheese-Loving Porkers

Any pasty-faced, rotund women who live in or near Minnesota and/or Wisconsin are certain to be of German ancestry. Although the Hindu prays to the cow, these people pray to what comes out of the cow: mainly milk fat in the form of cheese (although they also love veal, which technically comes out of a cow, too).

Midwestern Cheese-Loving Porkers are fiercely patriotic. They're generous and family-oriented but have absolutely no feel for interior decorating. We found that only Thai-Americans have less aptitude when it comes to knowing where to put things in a home.

MCLPs love the Packers, Jesus, and their mothers (in that order). Some of them might even slide a nice, juicy bratwurst in between Jesus and their mothers (figuratively speaking, of course).

7. Irish-Americans

A glamorous ethnic group that transformed themselves from gutter-crawling drunks all the way to president of the United States . . . and then back to gutter-crawling drunks.

When they first arrived here, many immigrants from all over the world became deeply depressed due to a lack of money, opportunity, and status. It's not surprising that they turned to drink for solace—and the Irish were no exception. Things have really improved for them though, so it's a little surprising that Bill Murray continues to drink.

Their reputation as heavy drinkers has crossed into all facets of American life. It's even a source of humor, as in this joke:

Q: What's the difference between an Irishman and an alcoholic?

A: The spelling.

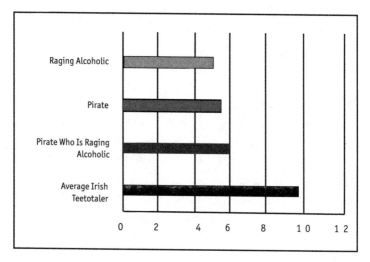

Drinks Per Day
Irish Males Vs. Others

Irish Catholic versus Irish Protestant

In Ireland, this distinction can be a matter of life and death. Here, it is less important. As long as they can imitate their grandparents' accent, they can always pick up women in bars. In Ireland, Irish Catholics root for Celtic while Irish Protestants root for Rangers. In America, all the Irish root for the Celtics and nobody (except for George W. Bush) roots for the Rangers.

Physical Characteristics

- Fair-skinned
- Ruddy complexion
- Tend to wear wool fisherman's sweaters even in summer
- Medium to small reproductive organs (Hey, not just penises! They have small ovaries, too!)

Food

Although not known for their culinary achievements (it's hard to operate a stove when you're plastered), the Irish have contributed several items to this country's food repertoire.

- **The pickled egg.** Timothy Connolly consumed 123 pickled eggs at the 1986 World Series. The Red Sox famously lost to the Mets, but Timmy won the hearts and minds of Irish-Americans everywhere.

- **The potato.** To our great surprise we discovered that the Irish actually invented the potato. Although you would think that a group who have worshipped this tuber for generations would be able to find something interesting to do with it.

- **Bangers.** Bangers are not members of the Irish street gang the Westies. They are actually sausages. It should be noted that the sausages are much more deadly than the Westies ever were.

- **Corned beef and cabbage.** Why this dish was brought over from the old country is impossible to understand. The Irish left behind the oppressive English, the foul weather, and the poor orthodontia—couldn't they have ditched this muck, too? Although, in the defense of Irish-Americans, corned beef and cabbage is an improvement over its first incarnation: corned rooster and dirty socks.

Sports

The Irish love sports. And even more than sports, the Irish love fighting over their favorite sports teams. In fact, the Irish love sports more than sex (although not as much as drinking). Please refer to the results of the Irish-American phone survey listed below.

Do you prefer having sex or watching sports?

Prefer having sex: 22%
Prefer watching sports: 36%*
Prefer having sex while watching sports: 42%
Who wants a beer?: 100%

*Included in this number are Catholic priests who insisted that watching naked boys play leapfrog was a sport.

Jobs

Although Irish-Americans can now be found in nearly all professions (except for dentistry), they still have a strong presence in the following occupations:

- Cops
- Bartenders
- Priests
- Firemen
- Belligerent Drunks

Geographical Patterns

Irish-Americans are found mostly in urban areas, where the need for cops, bartenders, priests, firemen, and drunks is much greater than in the countryside. In Boston after a Red Sox game, you can't help but stumble over one. If the Sox won, you have a chance of making it to your car in one piece. If the Sox lost, you should probably hang out near the security area until eight to ten hours after the final out.

Nesting Patterns

Irish-Americans tend to live in apartments and suburban single-family dwellings. Among Irish Catholics, a cross and a painting of Jesus are nearly always somewhere in the house.

In older specimens, there will most likely also be a photo of JFK on the wall. If they are hard-core old-school Irish, JFK will be slightly above Jesus but below the poster advertising Guinness stout.

Famous Irish-Americans
- Buster Keaton
- James Cagney
- John Wayne
- Jack Nicholson
- Lucky Charms leprechaun
- Grace Kelly
- Kermit the Frog (on his mother's side)

8. Polish-Americans

Polish-Americans have been singled out as being on the low end of the intelligence scale. Witness this common anecdote:

Q: Where do Polacks hide their armies?

A: Up their sleevies.

See, the implication here is that Polish people are stupid. And that's just not true. Polish people are no stupider than the rest of the people who hail from Eastern Europe (and parts of Oklahoma).

This erroneous and cruel reputation is more a function of self-induced separateness than any true lack of intelligence. Polish-Americans have tended to hold on to traditions and customs from the old country (including their native language). Other groups perceived their desire to still speak Polish as an inability to learn English, and the stereotype was created. So, let's make this clear once and for all—Polish people are not stupid. Except for the ones from Krakow.

Geographic Patterns

Poles live in major Eastern and Midwestern cities. Because of their thick trunks and legs, many Polish-American women stay away from the coasts, beaches, and public pools. (This is also why you never see Meryl Streep in a bathing suit.)

Nesting Patterns

Poles live in homes that are just like what the Pope would live in if he had no money. They are adorned with ornate chairs and paintings and religious icons. They are also filled with gaudy knick-knacks purchased at the 99-cent store. Basically, their homes look as if they were decorated by a drunk priest and a confused whore. Also, their houses always smell like ham.

Famous Poles

- Stan Musial
- Jerzy Kosinski
- Mike Peniskawolksi (changed surname to Ditka)
- Liberace (lost surname altogether)
- Kielbasa Karl (little-known sausage mascot who died of trichinosis)

9. French-Americans

Of all the Western European nations that saw their citizenry cross the Atlantic, the French had the fewest émigrés. And we're not complaining—trust us. A couple of French guys can ruin a good thing for everyone. But we do have a handful of French-Americans scurrying about within our borders. Here's a sampling.

A. Cajuns

Many French settled in Louisiana thinking that it was still French-owned. Little did they know their fellow countrymen sold the area to the Spanish, thereby yanking the étouffée right out from under their feet.

These disappointed French folk settled in mosquito-laden swamps, did some power inbreeding, and threw anything that moved into a pot and ate it. This is now known as the Cajun food you pay so much for at all the fancy hot spots.

It's not hard to spot a Cajun:

- They wear suspenders at all times
- They laugh and sing and have a real love for life
- They laugh and sing while raping and murdering tourists lost in the bayou

B. Rich Euro Club Kids

While not all Rich Euro Club Kids are French, most of them are. And the ones who aren't pretend to be. New York– or L.A.-based, they are young, rich, and bilingual. Their moms are beautiful interior decorators, and their fathers own châteaux in the Loire Valley.

They can't help but show off their knowledge of food and wine, and each has tasted a butter or brandy that is much, much better than any butter or brandy that you could ever hope to taste.

None of them needs to work, yet they all have impossibly glamorous jobs in finance and "the arts." They vacation in the Caribbean or the Swiss Alps and have lots and lots of sex with incredibly beautiful people.

As annoying as the Cajuns are, it's really the Rich Euro Club Kids who make everyone hate the French.

10. Russian-Americans

Russian-Americans are a relatively new group (except for the ones who were smart enough to get the hell out of Russia when the revolution started). They tend to inhabit the outer boroughs of New York and Chicago. Brighton Beach, New York, is a hard-core Russki town, with more vodka and smoked fish consumed there per capita than anywhere else on the planet.

The RAs have kept a relatively low profile, although younger generations are making their mark in the fields of tennis, modeling, and weapons-dealing. Here's a brief array of some subsets of the Russian-American.

A. Vodka-Loving Stalin Haters

Most Russians love vodka. And most Russians hate Stalin. Therefore, most Russians fall into this category. Interestingly, there are many similarities between this group and Cuban Rum-Loving Castro Haters. If you get these two groups in a room together, look out! They'll spend the whole day railing against Communism, plotting governmental overthrow, and getting hammered.

Vodka-Loving Stalin Haters tend to sing songs in Russian when they're drunk. Along with Gay Urban Professionals, they also are the major customers of steam baths. In a small neighborhood in San Francisco, Gay Russian Vodka-Loving Stalin Haters have actually created a twenty-four-hour steam bath/vodka bar. We sent one of our assistant researchers in there to check it out, but we never heard from him again.

B. Female Tennis Stars

Maria Sharapova, Anna Kournikova, Maria Kirilenko, Anastasia Miskina . . . Why are the only really pretty female tennis players Russian? Who cares? The important thing is that most of them become American citizens so we get to claim them on our census forms. Also, you can see their underwear.

C. Anorexic Supermodels

Pretty Russian-Americans who fail to develop tremendous tennis skills can always fall back on an exciting career as coked-out fashion models. These lovely ladies are tall, thin, beautiful, and wear extremely expensive, staggeringly soft leather. Generally speaking, they will not be found outside of New York, Miami, or Los Angeles unless they are in the desert, draped over a sports car shooting a commercial.

D. Young Oil Tycoons

YOTs live predominantly in New York (or at least have bought multimillion-dollar apartments there, even if they're always in Gstaad). They fly on private jets, consume the most expensive wines and food, and generally live the way Bill Gates would live if he weren't such a nerdy wimp.

11. The Southern Redneck

The Southern Redneck would have been higher up the White color scale if his neck weren't so red.

For an excellent survey of the Redneck subgenre, please see the collected writings, CDs, and DVDs of noted sociologist Jeff Foxworthy. Some of his insights prove invaluable in understanding the species. Just don't expect any of it to be funny.

12. The Appalachians

Originally of Scottish, English, and German heritage (although you'll never get them to admit it), Appalachians are a prime example of devolution, with each successive generation becoming worse off than the previous one. While once they were kings, circumstantial evidence suggests that an Appalachian baby was recently born with a partial shell on its back.

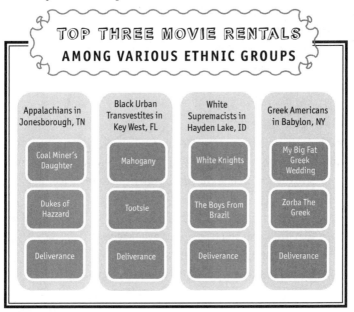

TOP THREE MOVIE RENTALS
AMONG VARIOUS ETHNIC GROUPS

Appalachians in Jonesborough, TN	Black Urban Transvestites in Key West, FL	White Supremacists in Hayden Lake, ID	Greek Americans in Babylon, NY
Coal Miner's Daughter	Mahogany	White Knights	My Big Fat Greek Wedding
Dukes of Hazzard	Tootsie	The Boys From Brazil	Zorba The Greek
Deliverance	Deliverance	Deliverance	Deliverance

Appalachian Character Traits

They enjoy:

- Fiddle playing
- Tobacco spitting
- Coal mining
- Cornholing
- Strip-mining
- Stripping in a coal mine

Differences between the Southern Redneck and the Appalachian

Although many lump them into one big "cracker barrel," there are several important distinctions between these two genetic cousins. (And by *cousins* we mean people who have sex with each other.)

The Redneck actually takes pride in his "otherness." He is not necessarily dirt-poor. In most cases, although he has probably felt up his sister, he knows where to draw the line.

The Appalachian is so poor that, for dessert, he makes Mississippi mud pie with real mud. Not a believer in foreplay, he doesn't waste his time feeling up his sister; he just goes right for the goods.

13. Greek-Americans

Greek-Americans have a great ability to "hide" among other ethnic groups (especially Italian-Americans and Jews). Here are some broad strokes that define the Greek-American experience:

- They dominate the diner business
- They will offer you baklava on every occasion
- They frequently smell of anise
- Deep down they all want to have sex with young men

BONUS SECTION

No Coke, Pepsi!

According to estimates, 90 percent of the quintessential "American" diners in the New York metropolitan area are owned by Greek-Americans. Nobody really knows how this dominance began or why, although we have a theory. Greece is considered the cradle of Western civilization. So, anyone who could spawn three thousand years of poetry, music, and art ought to be able to kick ass at making some fried eggs and bacon.

Famous Greeks in America
- Jennifer Aniston
- Michael Chiklis
- Kelly Clarkson
- Tina Fey
- Telly Savalas
- Pete Sampras
- John Stamos
- George Stephanopoulos
- Telly Savalas (he gets mentioned twice because, let's face it, he's the Greekiest)

Random Greek Survey

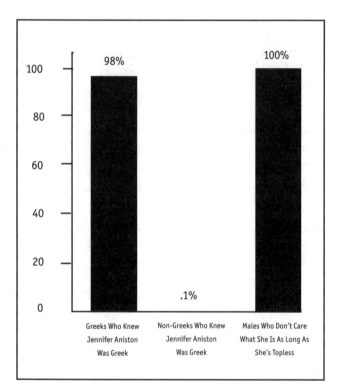

Food

- Olives
- Olive oil
- Olive bread
- Feta cheese (with a little olive oil sprinkled on top)

14. Jews

Are Jews an ethnicity or are they merely a ragtag collection of different ethnicities following a common religious philosophy? The answer: we don't know and we don't really care. We've written a section about them and we're including it in the book no matter what.

While still a small minority of total residents of the United States, the Jews have a disproportionately large public profile since either they control the media or lots of people just complain that they control the media, thereby placing them at the forefront of the media and making it easier for them to control it. Also, they make good rye bread.

The Jewish species has many subsets, including:

A. The Northeastern Jew

Perhaps the most interesting quality of the Northeastern Jew is that he spends a great deal of his time traveling, making travel plans, or working to afford a trip to Florida. Why the Northeastern Jew doesn't simply move to Florida and stay there is a matter of much conjecture. Probably Florida is too full of Florida Jews for the Northeastern Jews to settle there permanently.

With the Jews arriving in Florida around the same time as the Midwestern Snowbirds, annual potential for conflict exists between these two disparate groups. Fortunately, our research indicates that conflict is usually averted—except on weekend evenings at popular discount restaurants and when battling over tee times at public golf courses.

A smaller subset of Jews live in Florida and travel periodically to the Northeast, but these are mostly accountants for Colombian cocaine cartels.

B. The Anti-Semite Semite

Fully culturally assimilated, the Anti-Semite Semite vocationally takes professional advantage of his or her "Jewishness" but is vocally critical of the religion and its customs. The Anti-Semite Semite invariably marries outside his faith in a blatant attempt to enrage his parents. They are suitably enraged, until he gets a divorce, has a religious reawakening, and marries the rabbi's daughter—just as his parents always planned.

C. The Preppy Jew

Many Jews go to prep schools, but not all of them are Preppy. These Jews have to buy the Izods, distress the khakis, and clench their jaws shut just like the other Preppies. However, to achieve full-fledged "preppiness," this group has to go that extra mile. They really have to work hard to learn how to sail. And they creatively tweak their surnames for that added Preppy appeal. So, if you meet a yacht captain wearing madras shorts and Top-Siders whose last name is Kingsley, Morgan, or Burns . . . there's a pretty good chance there's some Jewishness going on.

This kind of deep-tissue assimilation is often frowned upon, but who are we to judge? Indian shape-shifters turned themselves into animals. Murray Rothstein turned himself into Sumner Redstone. Live and let live, you know what we mean?

D. The Jewish American Princess

So much has been written about this subspecies that we almost didn't bother researching it. We're glad we did, however, because we made a startling discovery: the Jewish American Princess is extinct! Somewhere between the disappearance of the Valley Girl and the death of the Grunge Chick, the Jewish American Princess just vanished without a trace. And we looked *all over* the mall.

15. White Supremacists

Somewhat surprisingly, one of the lowest rungs on the sliding scale of Whiteness belongs to the White Supremacists. While they pride themselves on their Whitey Whiteness, most White Supremacists are actually darker than many Browns, Blacks, and Yellows. Obviously we wouldn't tell them this to their faces, but it's an immutable ethnic fact.

Relatively simple creatures, the White Supremacists' main characteristics are a deluded sense of racial identity and the belief that there should be only one constitutional amendment (the second one).

They tend to migrate to small domiciles at the far ends of unpaved roads and are extremely self-sufficient. At the most recent Idaho White-Power Weekend Retreat and Chili Cook-Off, a new record was set. Darby Dinkelacher of Billings, Montana, killed, skinned, and ate a raccoon in under six minutes. Obviously this would have taken longer if he'd cooked it.

White Supremacists don't go to movies much, they shy away from techno dance clubs, and there's little chance you'll see them at a Jay-Z concert—unless they're casing the place to firebomb it.

As an interesting aside to any discussion of White Supremacists, it should be noted that most serial killers are White as well. Conservative estimates say that 87 percent of all serial killers are White. Also, 89 percent of serial killers eat their prey. So, by transitivity of equalities, White people are cannibals. Interesting.

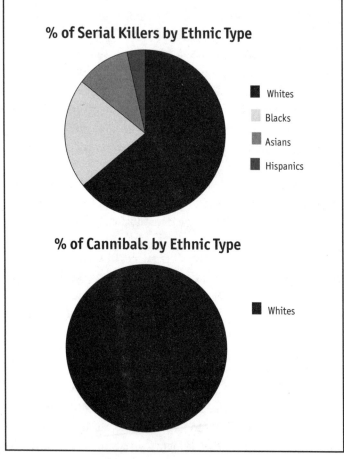

Science doesn't lie. Most serial killers are White. Most serial killers eat their victims. Therefore, most White people are cannibals. An interesting side note: cannibals who feast on Asians claim to be hungry for more human flesh in about an hour.

16. Italian-Americans

Many of you may question why Italian-Americans appear at the very bottom of the White chapter. And if you're Italian and reading this, you're probably calling "someone you know" to have us whacked.

But we're just following the results of our comprehensive study on the sliding scale of Whiteness. And it's not as if this information isn't already out there. As Chuck Nice, a noted DJ, comedian, and all-around talking head once said, "Italians are ni*&ers with short memories."

And if you don't want to take Mr. Nice's word for it, then check out the book *Are Italians White?* by Jennifer Guglielmo and Salvatore Salerno. Since we didn't read the book, we're not 100-percent sure of the answer. But the prevailing theory that we got from the Amazon reviews is that Italy's proximity to Africa has profoundly altered Italians' racial and ethnic identities. And we aren't just trying to stir the pot filled with gravy, *gabagool,* and *sausich*—we promise.

Whatever they are—Black, White, or burnt sienna—Italian-Americans have added a tremendous amount to our culture. Where would this great nation be without organized trash pickup and pizza?

Geographical Distribution

Originally settling in New York and San Francisco, Italian-Americans are now being forced out of their inner-city enclaves by more recent immigrant groups. Take New York's famed Little Italy: it's now more like Little Shanghai, with parts of it looking more like Little Place Where Only Billionaires Live. Rao's, the famous Italian eatery in Spanish Harlem, used to be the centerpiece of a thriving

Italian neighborhood. Now it's just Rao's, the famous (and only) Italian eatery in Spanish Harlem.

Nesting Habits

Most Italian-Americans who moved out to the suburbs are proud of their homes. Remember how Tony Soprano used to love showing off his pool? And why shouldn't they be proud? Most of those houses have more stonework than the Vatican. And their lawns! The Vatican *wishes* it had a lawn that nice!

Fashion

Although most of the world looks to Milan for avant-garde fashion, somehow the fashion gene has been mutated by the transatlantic migration. In this country, Italian-Americans dress the way Stevie Wonder would if he dressed himself in a closet filled with Yankee jerseys and tube socks. Take a walk around Lodi, New Jersey, for example. You'll most likely see:

- Large, gaudy pinkie rings
- Ties that match the color of the shirt, the socks, the underwear, and the Cadillac
- Socks so paper-thin that you can see through them
- Ankles so hairy you wish they were covered by thicker socks

All of these outfits apply to men and women, by the way.

Common Misperceptions and Stereotypes

• **Italian-Americans are all involved in organized crime**
Untrue! As much as they'd like to still dominate this sector of our

economy, the Chinese and South Americans have basically taken over. Look for a network series about a Latino organized-crime family very soon. It'll be exactly like *The Godfather*—just replace all the mentions of *cannoli* with references to *flan*.

• All Italians talk with their hands
Untrue! Most do, and sometimes they can be confused with homeless schizophrenics when you're walking through Boston's North End. We know for a fact that not all Italians talk with their hands because our IT guy is Italian, and, well, he doesn't talk with his hands.

By the way, if you want to see some really emotive conversations, chat up a Sicilian. When Sicilians get a head of steam going, they'll kick off their shoes and start talking with their feet.

• Italian-Americans don't like homosexuals
Untrue! Italian-Americans *hate* homosexuals. This is an important distinction to make if you happen to be gay and you find yourself on the Jersey shore one hot August night.

Dr. Leonard Ripps, a noted sociologist and not-so-noted trapeze artist, conducted a lengthy study with shocking conclusions. He discovered that the combination of Catholicism, skintight T-shirts, excessive consumption of manicotti, and the presence of overbearing mothers has caused all Italian-American men to secretly be gay. Which, obviously, is why they're so hard on the homosexuals. We tried to reach Dr. Ripps to discuss his results, but he was not reachable. His landlady said that some guys wearing wifebeaters who smelled of Aqua Velva took him away in a powder blue Lincoln Continental.

Famous Italian-Americans

- Frank Sinatra (Obviously there are hundreds more, but nobody touches Frank, you know what we mean?)

Infamous Italian-Americans

- Al Capone
- John Gotti
- Vinny "the Chin" Gigante
- Sammy "the Bull" Gravano
- Annette Funicello

Food

Food is very important to Italian-Americans. They make it, they eat it, they throw it around the room when they get mad. Of course, food is important to every ethnic group, but with Italians, it's like a religion—except priests hardly ever molest chicken *scarpariello*.

Pizza. Salami. Pasta. The list goes on and on. And although the Chinese and Italians fight over the origins of pasta, we come down on the side of the Italians. Frankly, this is a no-brainer. How could the Chinese have invented pasta if *pasta* is an Italian word?

Italian-Americans celebrate their love of food at religious feasts that honor saints and phony-baloney people they make up to be saints just so they can celebrate their love of food at religious feasts. At these feasts, you can get your palm read, your ass pinched, and your wallet thinned, all while you stuff your face with a sausage-and-pepper sandwich the size of a newborn (BTW, they both come out with the same amount of pain).

But the highlight of these feasts is the sacred "fried dough"— a magical culinary concoction that has been handed down from generation to generation through the ages. The recipe to this delicacy is usually shrouded in mystery. We disguised a Hechinger operative with a mesh shirt and lots of chest and back hair to infiltrate a kitchen at the Festa di Italia in Spokane, Washington. He was almost murdered, but he escaped with the sacred secret. Enjoy.

RECIPE FOR FRIED DOUGH

    1. Take dough.

    2. Fry it.

    Buon appetito!

CHAPTER V

YELLOWS

The recent advent of political correctness has inadvertently caused people to shy away from certain perfectly innocuous scientific terms. One of these victims of the new age is *Yellow* as a modifier describing the panoply of Asian-derived ethnicities.

Now, obviously, when we say Yellow we're not talking about a Bart Simpson or a Big Bird yellow—that would be racially insensitive. We're just talking about the kind of Yellow you find throughout the Asian world—such as in Pikachu or those little egg-custard cups that you get at the dim sum restaurants.

Isn't it enough that scientists (like us) can no longer refer to the Asians as Orientals? Can't they leave our Yellow alone? It seems especially unfair when you consider that most scientists are Asian to begin with. If they're okay with it, shouldn't we all be?

While the history of the Asian world dates back for millennia, the history of America is relatively brief. Yellows have been important contributors to our national pupu platter almost since the beginning. The first Asians to come here were Chinese-Filipinos who settled in Mexico in the early 1700s, then worked their way north. That paved the way for millions more, many of whom helped build our railroad system, which no one uses anymore. Thanks anyway, though.

Asian-Americans are an extremely diverse group. For expediency we have simplified and categorized them into these general traits:

Physical Characteristics

• First of all, they're Yellow. Or at least they're as Yellow as White people are White, or Black people are Black. Brown people actually really are kind of Brown.

• The Chinese tend to be tallest; Filipinos the shortest. The Japanese and Koreans are the squattest, and Koreans have the largest heads. Almost all of them have black hair on their heads, and not much hair on their bodies. Also, they all think that Westerners smell like rancid beef.

Geographical Patterns

Asian-Americans, more than almost any other group, have settled in every part of North America. This predisposition to move around is precisely why the federal government wanted to round up all the Japanese-Americans in World War II.

The Asian-American diaspora has introduced all sectors of American society to the wonders of Asian culture. It's the reason that you can get good Peking duck in Sheboygan.

Yellows tend to live in big cities such as San Francisco and New York. But they also can be found in rural areas of Texas, Oklahoma, and Virginia, where they usually operate large farms. That's why the only items you can find in every market in America are potato chips and bok choy.

Some suburban towns are nearly 100 percent Asian. If you cannot afford to go to Shanghai for an authentic Asian experience, take a quick trip to Monterey Park, California, instead. In

Monterey Park, a completely Chinese bedroom community just east of L.A., not only is every sign in Mandarin, but spitting in public is encouraged and Irish people are considered well hung.

Here's how to tell if you live in an Asian-American neighborhood:

- Does the air smell of fish sauce and/or teriyaki?
- Do all of your neighbors leave their shoes outside their front door?
- Are there an inordinate number of garden centers and driving ranges close to your home?
- Are you Asian?

If the answer to one or more of these questions was yes or "Hai!" then your neighborhood is Yellow.

Nesting Patterns

The interiors of Yellow domiciles tend to be neat (except, obviously, for the homes of Filipinos, who rank just ahead of Appalachians in the category).

Without exception, every Yellow home has at least one rice cooker. In lower-class and middle-class homes, the rice cooker is a small household electrical appliance. In more affluent homes, the rice cooker will usually be a Guatemalan housekeeper.

Another essential ingredient of the Asian-American home is the karaoke machine. Also, there's usually a lot of sake and Johnnie Walker Black to get everyone loosened up enough to sing R. Kelly's "I Believe I Can Fly." This song works on many levels in the Asian community and is especially popular among chefs. (Just sing it in an Asian accent and you'll realize what we're talking about.)

Every Asian-American household will feature some kind of area where one can grow produce. This can range from a large vegetable farm in the back of the house to a small tomato plant in the back of the prison cell.

If Yellows have pets, these pets will usually be fish. For some reason dogs and cats tend not to stick around too long.

Mating Habits

Asian-Americans reproduce sparingly (except for Filipinos, who give the Latinos a run for their money). The reasons for their limited reproductivity are numerous. A perceived obsession with their relative infertility could be partly to blame (see recipe for shark-fin soup—guaranteed to make your wife conceive a male child or, at the very least, give you diarrhea).

Another possible explanation for limited mating is the stereotypical perception that Yellows are genetically inferior dancers. The Twyla Tharp Genome Project, however, completely debunked this theory when it proved conclusively that Whites are the worst dancers, especially Whites from New England.

For whatever reasons, some Asians are clearly less "productive" than other ethnicities. A classic archetype of this brand of Asian is embodied in the Passive Asian Male.

Passive Asian Male (PAM)

Not much has been written about the Asian-American male. You don't see many in Hollywood movies, professional sports, or ads in *Vanity Fair*. How many famous Asian male models can you name? Exactly. Even the models in Japanese porno magazines are White. Studies indicate that a reason for this, beyond the obvious racism, is the even more obvious fact that this isn't even true.

Empirically, Asian-American males do not score high on masculinity indices—Yao Ming and Jet Li notwithstanding.

Asian-Americans are perceived to be basically wimpy and non-confrontational. Hideki Matsui, for example, never gets mad no matter how far out of the zone a called strike might have been.

Whether it's the academic achievement, the propensity for playing the violin, the lack of body hair, or their living with their parents even after they get married—Asian males have a long row to hoe when it comes to hoeing the hos. In an ESPN/*Hustler* survey, hot chicks listed, in order of preference, the kinds of men with whom they would most like to have sex:

1. NBA players
2. Rock stars
3. Hollywood stars
4. Colombian drug lords
5. A horse
6. Retarded Appalachians
7. Hairless Asian-American violin players who live at home with their parents

This aversion to hooking up with Asian men may be changing, however. John Cho, the nerdy, hairless PAM who stars in the *Harold & Kumar* movies, may have started a small Yellow sexual revolution all by himself.

Yellow Buying Habits
Asian-Americans buy:

- Rice
- Scotch
- German cars

Asian-Americans don't buy:

- Razor blades
- Dog food
- Extra-large condoms

Speech Patterns

Most Asian-Americans speak English better than everyone in the state of Alabama, although obviously that's not saying much. In truth, the long-standing emphasis on academics has enabled Yellows to achieve tremendous educational success. Among the newer arrivals, and the old guard who are simply stuck in their ways, we came across many language issues. Some of this is due to intrinsic dialectal differences. Some of it is just a way to keep the "White devil" on his toes.

The following is a conversation we overheard while waiting in line at a Bank of America in San Francisco:

Chinese Woman: Why evelytime I come here, you give me difflent amount of dollar for yuan?

Caucasian Bank Teller: Fluctuations.

Chinese Woman: Fluck you White devils, too!

This exchange could have gone south in a heartbeat as the Chinese woman was furious and brandishing a fistful of ginger root. Fortunately, cooler heads prevailed and she was merely arrested after being repeatedly tasered by local cops.

Hobbies/Recreation/Sports

Asian-Americans have not traditionally excelled at the big four American sports (baseball, football, basketball, hockey). They do love their leisure time, however, and have achieved greatness in other forms of recreation. Here is a brief list of sports in which Asian-Americans stand out:

- Table tennis
- Studying
- Clipping fingernails on crowded airplanes
- Gambling
- Cutting in line
- Spitting in public (scheduled to be an Olympic event in 2012)

Asian-American Subspecies

The simplest way to subdivide the vast morass of Asian-Americans is to group them according to their ancestral country of origin. These generalized observations are valid—although they're becoming less so every day as Asian-American subgroups are intermingling more and more. That is to say, Chinese-Americans are marrying Korean-Americans and having little ChikoAm kids who will, in turn, marry Japanese-Americans. Before you know it, there will just be a lot of Americans running around and we'll be out of a job.

Chinese-Americans

The original Asian-Americans, granddaddy to them all. All the pleasant Asian stereotypes (hard workers, good at laundry, excellent violin players) began with the Chinese immigrants.

The unpleasant stereotypes did, too (bad drivers, small penises, enough with the violins already). The Chinese-Americans universally have a sunny disposition and are enthusiastic members of all walks of national life. A careful look into their eyes, however, reveals a still-simmering resentment at having been forced to lay all those railroad tracks. They are all secretly proud that their motherland is now kicking America's butt at everything.

Culturally, Chinese-Americans can be broken down into three distinct groups:

Assimilated

They seamlessly blend in with society at large. Ethnic individuality only surfaces when local church groups or neighborhood associations insist on speaking loudly and slowly to them. At these times they angrily tell these people that they're neither deaf nor stupid. Then they remind them how the Asians destroyed them on the bell curve.

In fact, according to recent studies, Asian IQs are ten points higher than those of other ethnic groups—although Asians living in Mississippi tend to score below average. Their children know how to play the violin but keep it on the down low. The assimilated Chinese drive well and can even be found going quickly in the passing lane.

Recently, progress has been made in the world of sports. Unsubstantiated reports have second- and third-generation Chinese-Americans playing tennis, basketball, and soccer. There was one reported high school football player of Chinese descent, but he was killed instantly on the first day of practice.

Semi-assimilated

They still celebrate the traditional Moon Festival and speak in charming faraway accents. They operate successful restaurants, dry cleaners, or camera wholesalers (in areas where the Orthodox Jews don't have a monopoly on camera wholesaling). The semi-assimilated Chinese are cautious drivers, known to clog up the middle lane. Their children play the violin extremely well, and you will be forced to listen to them play the violin extremely well all the time. Nearly all semi-assimilated Chinese-American families have a piano in their house, regardless of whether someone actually plays it.

Still Chinese

No matter how long certain Chinese-Americans have been in this country—even if it's been five generations—some of them are just still Chinese. They wear those little slippers everywhere and insist on not understanding what you're saying, even though you know they took AP English in high school. These hard-core traditionalists don't even bother with the violin. They play that weird guitar-looking thing with two strings made out of a turtle shell.

And woe unto you if you get stuck behind them on the highway. They treat the gas pedal as if it were made out of avian bird flu (which they also spread by hawking up phlegm at the drop of a hat and spitting it out in the most inappropriate places—the subway, next to you on a plane, during someone's wedding ceremony . . .).

Hechinger Study of Drive Times
for Various Ethnic Groups
(in Hours)

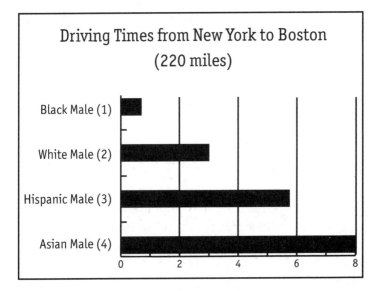

(1) Chased by state troopers and police helicopter—got there in 37 minutes

(2) Stopped four times to fill up Hummer

(3) 1969 Datsun broke down, then lost tire on 91. Arrived in tow truck

(4) Never arrived, rumored to still be lost in Westchester

Japanese-Americans

The most prosperous of the Yellows, Japanese-Americans have, in only sixty years, gone from being locked up in internment camps to controlling a large percentage of the nation's banking, real estate, and sushi institutions. They are also a force to be reckoned with in the worlds of gardening, high technology, and judo. Their phenomenal success is all the more impressive when you consider that the Japanese-Americans are disliked and resented by all the other Asians because of Japan's endless legacy of imperialism and abuse (although that may be another reason why they have done so well in America).

Assimilated

The assimilated Japanese-Americans are the least obtrusively Asian of all your Yellows. They frequently marry White people— they especially like Midwesterners—so that the second and third generations begin to defy traditional physical stereotypes. Rumor has it that Hillary Rodham Clinton is one-eighth Japanese, which may help explain her relentless work ethic and her staggering dexterity with chopsticks.

Semi-assimilated

More recent arrivals from the Land of the Rising Sun have blended in well with the rest of American society, but they still insist on sending their children to school with brown paper bags stuffed with sushi and plum paste–filled rice balls. The children, well on their way to becoming fully assimilated, trade these dishes with their friends in exchange for baloney sandwiches and Cheetos.

Still Japanese

Many Japanese-Americans—especially really rich ones on the West Coast whose families have been here for over 150 years—still refuse to speak English without woefully mispronouncing their *l*'s and *r*'s. They do this to maintain a sense of ethnic Japaneseness. That's also why they only drive Lexuses and why, when they've had a few too many sakes, they grumble, "Someday soon Hawaii will be part of Japan, the way the Shinto gods intended."

Asian-American Hate Index of Other Asian-Americans

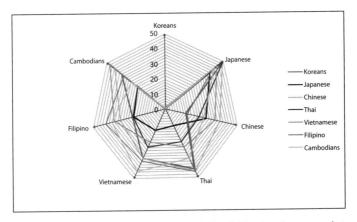

We actually have no idea how to read this. Basically all Asian-American groups hate Japanese-Americans . . . apparently even the Japanese.

It must also be noted that the only people who can actually read this chart are the Japanese.

Another interesting sidebar to this study is that if you cut along the lines and fold the paper along the axis, it makes a pretty origami swan.

=== BONUS SECTION ===

The Japanese-Jewish Connection

Although Jews are most regularly associated with Asian-American culture by way of Sunday-night dinner at Chinese restaurants, a more direct link has become increasingly common: the marriage of Japanese-American women to Jewish males. That's right, it's a whole new kind of JAP.

Why is this? Our records indicate two factors are responsible here. One: the groups have profound cultural and behavioral similarities. For example, they both respect:

- Education
- Becoming doctors
- Luxury cars
- A good bargain
- The threat of internment

The second reason is sociological: as Jewish-American females became more independent and less submissive, Jewish males said, "Screw it. I don't need this shit!" And they went out and found some even more submissive women to settle down with.

Although our sampling was small (Jerry Nathanson and his wife, Kiko, and another couple we heard about in Boston), we do feel that this is a significantly increasing trend.

The joke may be on these Jewish males, however. For all their seeming submissiveness, if you've ever tried to play through a foursome of Japanese ladies on the golf course, you know what the pulsing, bloody heart of aggression looks like.

Korean-Americans

Don't look now, but the Koreans are taking over everything. We don't want to alarm you, but that is their predominant ethnic stereotype (and it's true!). Korean-Americans are the fastest-rising subset in the Yellow group. Their specialty is sneakily buying up stores/products/chains that you have no idea are run by Koreans, then making themselves indispensable.

For example, did you know that Korean-Americans are in complete control of the tastiest fried-chicken restaurants in this country? They are! Like all the Asian-Americans, Koreans are extremely hardworking—but their sneakiness dovetails well with the traditional American respect for entrepreneurship and corruption. So keep an eye on these guys—the twenty-first century may well be their time to shine.

Assimilated

Prominent in the financial fields, the assimilated Koreans are almost indistinguishable from the rest of the population except that their names are always Park.

They are also prevalent in the fields of nursing, IT, engineering, and animation. As in almost everything else, they think their animation skills exceed those of their natural rivals, the Japanese. As in everything else, however, Japanese animation wins hands down.

Assimilated Korean-Americans love gambling, smoking, and drinking Johnnie Walker Black—but then again, who doesn't?

Two Korean Subspecies

In exploring Los Angeles and New York, our researchers came across two specific subspecies of the Korean-American.

Koreatown Club-Scene Chick (KCSC)

With one high heel in Asian pop culture and one in American, these sexy young things consume stylish cocktails, wear lots of black, and highlight their exotic and sensual "Asian" features. It is their last acting-out before they inevitably settle down with a Korean dude and instantly turn into their mothers.

UCLA Korean Gangsta Wannabe (UKGW)

Although *The Fast and the Furious* did much to improve the Asian male's rep, he still has a long way to go. The UKGW comes from a middle-class background, is highly educated and law-abiding, and loves his parents more than he cares to admit.

Because of this, he overcompensates by assuming the guise of a gangsta with oversize clothes, baseball hat askew, and copious bling. Add to this a "tuned" Japanese street racer and you have one bad dude . . . who is usually in bed by eleven to study for his physics test the next day.

Semi-assimilated

Prominent in the appliance and automobile industries, semi-assimilated Koreans stand out slightly because they play more golf than busy people should be able to. Their women wear large, brightly colored visors on the golf course, and their men gamble, smoke, and drink a lot—but they never seem to go bankrupt, get lung cancer, or get rowdy.

Still Korean

Prominent in the twenty-four-hour convenience-store industry, the Still Korean Koreans bury pots of kimchi in their backyards in St. Louis and bristle at Kim Jong Il jokes. Their women rarely speak unless spoken to, and their men gamble, smoke, and drink so much that you can't help but wonder how anything actually gets done in Korea.

In most cases, even with those who have been in North America for twenty years, one spouse will not speak English.

PDAs (public displays of affection) are not encouraged, although electronic PDAs are. Computer-mapping software indicates that most Korean couples stop kissing after the age of thirty-five.

The Rest

Vietnamese

Vietnamese-Americans have been riding a crest of sympathy for over forty years. America realizes that it screwed over Vietnam royally, and we've been cutting its descendants slack ever since that ghastly snafu. The Vietnamese-Americans have this national guilt to thank for their tremendous successes—especially at the poker table.

Yes, many of the most successful poker pros today are Vietnamese-Americans. These men and women win thousands of hands that anyone else would have lost solely because the people against whom they are playing don't have the heart to give a Vietnamese another brutal beating. That's why Scotty Nguyen lives in a mansion in Vegas with sports cars and pet monkeys—because Lyndon Johnson carpet bombed Hanoi.

Although one might assume that a Vietnamese speaking French is showing off, the reality is that they were initially colonized by the French. This did not work out so well for the Vietnamese, although it did create a cuisine that combines the best of Asian and French cooking.

Vietnamese-Americans also:

- Are able to ride a moped at birth
- Do not like being asked if they are Korean or Chinese
- Are not-so-secretly creating a worldwide nail-salon empire

Thais

The Thai-American was enjoying a quiet life and low national profile until the rest of the country realized how delicious pad thai noodles are. Also, that tsunami kind of put them on the map (even while it took many of them off the map, so to speak).

Thai-Americans are held to unrealistically high sexual standards due to the deservedly perverse reputation of the citizens of Bangkok. But, let's face it, if you're living in a gated community in Ocala, Florida, the only thing you're doing with Ping-Pong balls is playing Ping-Pong.

Tiger Woods is perhaps the most popular Thai in the world. Thais in general have a predisposition for golf and for Buicks, so Tiger fits right in. Of course, his father was Black and his wife is Swedish—so he fits into pretty much every chapter of this book (much like Cameron Diaz).

Filipinos

Considered the Blacks of Asian-Americans (or, conversely, the Mexicans of Indonesia), Filipino-Americans (or Flip-Ams) have the largest penises of all the Yellows.*

---

*Our only evidence for this is when Ling Ling Marcos whipped his wiener out in the parking lot of Vendome Liquors in Sherman Oaks. We didn't ask him to, by the way, but we're doing serious scientific research here, so we felt obligated to take a look. Yikes. (It should also be noted that we received no answer to our numerous requests to take a look at Yao Ming's ding-dong.)

Filipino-Americans also tend to be poorer and less ambitious, but enjoy life more than most of the other Asian-American groups—perhaps their general contentment can be tied to Ling Ling's special gift.

Filipino-Americans tend to be extremely musical and are inordinately proud that one of their own is in the Black Eyed Peas.

Cambodians

Cambodian-Americans don't have a long history in North America, basically because they enjoyed their native paradise until civil war, repression, and genocide nearly destroyed their nation.

They came here starting in 1979, and like the Vietnamese they have endeared themselves to America because of their hard work and all of our guilt over what we put them through.

The Cambodian-American population is still small enough that their only predominant ethnic stereotype is that they're short and they eat dogs. Based on our extensive research, this turns out to be pretty accurate, although we did meet a guy named Rithipol who was almost six feet tall.

Laotians

We only discovered fifty-seven Laotian-Americans. They were all living in the same apartment complex in Oxnard, California. None of them spoke English or had fingernails. They did not appear to be friendly. We quickly continued north toward Santa Barbara.

CHAPTER VI

EXOTIC BREEDS

Look around you; if you see people of "mixed ancestry" and cannot quite figure out what they are . . . you're not alone. If you are alone and you see people of mixed ancestry, then you are either in dire need of medical attention or you're being haunted by ghosts.

This chapter is going to look at the numerous groups that just don't "fit" into the previous monochromatic ethnic classifications.

A. Eskimos

Alaska is even farther north than the Great White North, so, technically speaking, Eskimos are the Whitest of the Whites—which is ironic considering how dark they are. Eskimos originated in Asia and arrived at their present homeland by traversing an isthmus across the Bering Strait. The extreme weather conditions in Alaska limit the Eskimo's outdoor activities, which are pretty much reduced to:

- Watching your breath freeze
- Watching your pee freeze
- Attending sleddog races

- Attending sleddog funerals
- Trying to stay alive

Also, during the winter months when there can be as little as a half hour of daylight in each twenty-four-hour cycle, the entire Eskimo community has been known to play massive games of flashlight tag.

Nesting

One of the many skills that Eskimos have perfected over the years is building their homes . . . or igloos. When we first heard reports that these igloos are made out of snow, we laughed at this preposterous suggestion. Further research has, however, revealed that they really are made out of snow. Amazing! The record for building an igloo is thirty-eight minutes.*

How to Make an Igloo While Drunk

Step 1. Get drunk.

Step 2. Cut blocks from dry, hard snow, using a snow saw or large knife. Each block should be about three feet (1 m) long, fifteen inches (40 cm) high, and eight inches (20 cm) deep.

Step 3. Throw up.

*As a point of comparison, it took Minneapolis resident Randolph Thurston eight days to build a toolshed out of Fudgsicle sticks.

Step 4. Form a circle with blocks around the hole created where you cut out the blocks. Cut the circle in a spiral from the top of the last block to the ground ahead of the first block. This will make it easy to construct a dome.

Step 5. Shit your pants.

Step 6. Build up walls, overlapping the blocks and shaping them so that they lean inward. Put several blocks along one wall as a sleeping platform.

Step 7. Wonder why it smells so bad inside the igloo.

Step 8. The last block must initially be larger than the hole. Place the block on top of the igloo, then, from inside, shape and wiggle it to slot exactly into the hole.

Step 9. Forget to leave an opening in igloo. Trap yourself inside and die of suffocation.

Clothing

For obvious reasons, Eskimos wear many layers of warm clothes. These include brightly colored parkas made of squirrel, wolf, wolverine, and mink. Reindeer fur is reserved for special occasions such as a young man's first whale hunt and bar mitzvahs.

The Eskimo's Best Friend

The Eskimo's best friend is the Seal. The Seal's best friend is the Penguin. And the Penguin's best friend is the Joker—man, was Heath Ledger good in that movie.

Seals serve many purposes for the Eskimo, being used for:

- Food
- Clothing
- Fuel
- Condoms

And let's face it, if you've got food, clothing, fuel, and condoms, what more do you need? Our best friend is a dog, and what has he ever given us besides a steamy surprise in our slippers?

B. Hawaiians

Categorizing the Hawaiians is problematic. And don't just listen to us—the *Encyclopedia of American Ethnic Groups* says, "A particularly high rate of intermarriage between native Polynesian Hawaiians and immigrants has resulted in an increasing proportion of people whose ethnicity can be described as problematic." See? We didn't make *all* this stuff up.

Noted ethnic scholar and marble collector Dr. Richard Fedeli suggested, "Trying to classify Hawaiians is like trying to pick a hooker at the Bunny Ranch. It's extremely challenging, but fun."

Frankly, it's not so challenging for us. But that's just 'cause we love redheads.

Whatever their specific ethnicity, Hawaiians tend to be fun-loving, family-oriented, and in tune with nature. They also love surfing and hate tourists, no matter how nice they may act while you're checking in.

Hawaiian King Fun Fact

King Kamehameha, the greatest of the Hawaiian kings and the man responsible for uniting the Hawaiian islands, was fascinated by his own feces. He even had assistants carry his royal rectal rejects around in ornately carved wooden boxes.

In an effort to see whether this "ritual" is still relevant, we enlisted the help of the cabana boy at our hotel in Wailea. We had him wander around the beach with an engraved wooden box full of his own excrement, which he proudly displayed to everyone. Our research experiment ended before sufficient data was compiled when some drunken surfers stabbed the cabana boy to death. Our condolences to his family.

Food

Quite remarkably, Hawaiians have taken some of the most fertile ground on earth and the fine ethnic cuisines of a variety of cultures and used them to produce a cuisine that you would be embarrassed to feed to a rabid raccoon. Hawaiian "delicacies" include:

- *Poki* (not Gumby's friend, but a horrid mixture of dried salted fish)
- Taro root chips (our suggestion is to throw out the chips and eat the bag)
- SPAM (ham in a can! Congratulations, Hawaii! You suck!)

C. Rare Sightings

The following ethnic oddities have been spotted in small numbers throughout the United States.

- **Chifros**—(half-Chinese/half-Black) A happy, party-loving people, Chifros only get violent if you try to steal their spareribs
- **Jewnese**—(half-Jewish/half-Chinese) Inscrutably shrewd. Microscopic reproductive organs
- **Chinky-McDrinkys**—(half-Chinese/half-Irish) They drink, they smoke, they gamble, they'll press your shirts

D. Inbreeds

The Case against Inbreeding

From what we've observed in our studies and travels, the overwhelming trend in America is for ethnic groups to interbreed: Chinese with Whites, Colombians with Haitians, etc. This is the inescapable and wonderful result of living in a color-blind melting pot.

But some groups would argue that interbreeding is a mistake, and the only way to preserve an ethnicity's essence is to breed within your own. We're not interested in passing judgment on the choices made by others. However, we will simply point out that White Supremacists, the Amish, and Hasidic Jews all look exactly the same—and that scares us.

In the spirit of open-mindedness, allow us to present the counter to our argument as delineated in the groundbreaking paper "I Heart Inbreeding" by Drs. James, Janice, and Jessica Pelham (all of whom are brother and sister, father and daughter, and—surprisingly—members of the same handball team).

They found several advantages to inbreeding, which include:

- Inbreeding makes it easy to find someone to date
- Inbreeding keeps family heirlooms and possessions in the family
- Inbreeding makes Thanksgiving a lot more entertaining

Inbreed Identification Signs

Not that you necessarily need to fear Inbreeds, but just in case you do, here are some helpful hints on how to spot them:

- Inbreeds have pasty, sallow skin and wear thick glasses
- Inbreeds wear loose-fitting garments and smell like burnt toast
- Inbreeds run alligator-wrestling venues as well as Fortune 500 companies
- Watch out! Inbreeds are coming to get you!

CHAPTER VII

SPECIAL OCCASIONS, WEDDINGS, HOLIDAYS, FUNERALS

Holidays, celebrations, and special occasions are extremely important in the maintenance and continuation of the essence of an ethnic identity. For example, WASPs wouldn't have been able to keep their rich and vibrant culture alive through the ages if they didn't gather with family every Thanksgiving to drink and wife-swap.

These special times are also a way to get out of work, score some gifts, kiss pretty strangers, and be drunk in public without getting arrested (see New York's Puerto Rican Day Parade and Boston's Marathon Day for exceptions to this rule).

But in this day and age of mélange and confusion, it's hard to keep abreast of all of the customs and traditions celebrated by each ethnic group. Bringing Carolina pulled pork to a Ramadan party would probably not go over well. The same holds true for bringing a Muslim to a Carolina pork-pulling contest.

Because ethnic groups are commingling more than ever, we

feel it is important to have a basic knowledge of the customs and traditions of a wide variety of ethnic types. Generally speaking, holidays can be understood this way:

- If the holiday is celebrated by Latinos or the Irish, anticipate a tremendous amount of drinking, and the real possibility that you will get knifed.

- If the holiday is only celebrated by Latinos, then drinking will be followed by the firing of live ammunition into the air. This is true whether it's Cinco de Mayo or someone's first communion.

- If the holiday is celebrated by Whites and Blacks, then it will be celebrated by everybody. If the holiday is only celebrated by Whites, then it's probably St. Patrick's Day and you should hide indoors (even if you're Irish). If the holiday is only celebrated by Blacks, then it's Kwanzaa and you can ignore it (even if you're Black).

- If the holiday is only celebrated by Jews, then it's one of those Jewish holidays that Jews only pretend they're Jewish for so they can get out of work.

- If the holiday is celebrated by everyone *except* Jews, then it's Christmas. Buy your kids something nice.

Below is a "tip sheet" if you are invited to an event that is outside your ethnic background or sphere of knowledge.

What to Do If You're Invited to a Quinceañera Celebration

First, you should probably figure out what the heck you've been invited to. A quinceañera is like a coming-out party for a Latino girl, and it occurs on her fifteenth (*quince*) birthday. Occasionally, it coincides with a baby shower, too.

A lot of Latinos will be there, and they're not just there to park your car. Dress nicely with bright colors and flamboyant jewelry. Ladies, you should dress up, too.

Do not arrive on time. No one else will be there, and the hosts will make you run to the liquor store for booze. A half hour tardy is good, up to an hour late is acceptable.

If you are giving cash or a check as a gift, don't put the money down the young lady's dress or in her stockings—that's a great way to get nut-punched. And her father will probably be mad also.

What to Wear to a Rapper's Funeral

First things first: do you want to show somber respect? Or do you want to fit in? If you want to show respect, send a donation to the rapper's charity of choice. If you want to fit in, put on a $10,000 suit, a giant platinum pendant with your first initial on it, an oversize hat made of mink or otter fur, and fire up an eight ball—this is going to be an all-nighter. Expect the deceased to be buried with more gold than Tutankhamen. And don't act surprised if the casket is in the shape of the car the deceased was driving when he accidentally drove off the Throgs Neck Bridge while being shot at.

How to Behave at a Bar/Bat Mitzvah

This ceremony is a celebration of a Jewish adolescent's transformation to adulthood (even though the male will be a mama's boy until he is eighty).

Prepare to sit through hours of prayer and singing (snacks are frowned upon, although any type of mint or chewing gum is fine . . . as long as you have enough for the entire congregation).

Yarmulkes (skullcaps or Jew beanies) are optional, but you will be treated much nicer if you have one on.

At the party there will be a DJ. The DJ will be horrible. Stick around, though, the food is usually pretty good.

If You're Going to a New Year's Eve Party in the Midwest

A Midwestern New Year's Eve party will involve staring at a groaning board of casseroles (which is short for inedible leftovers covered with melted cheese). Out of every ten casseroles, only one will be fit for human consumption. *Do not* eat until you see what the "regulars" eat, then pounce. Exploration is not an option here. Save yourself for dessert; that's when the real eating begins.

If you want to avoid boredom, don't talk about cheese, sausage, the Packers, or lake trout.

If you want to avoid being beaten to death, don't talk about your displeasure with the Republican Party, global warming, or same-sex marriages.

Do compliment your hosts' miniature-wooden-clog collection. You don't even have to make sure they have one. Trust us—they have one.

At the stroke of midnight, instantly sprint out the front door. If you don't, you will get tongue-kissed by every six-hundred-pound Greta and Mildred in the joint.

An In-Depth Look: The Cajun Wedding

Cajun weddings are glorious events full of the kind of fun, warmth, and emotion that only occur when a brother and a sister get hitched.

The ceremony itself will be held in a church or reception hall or musky lean-to out by the alligator pens. In the past, if the justice of the peace was not present (or conscious), the couple could jump over a broom to certify their marriage. They've caught up with the times, of course; now if the justice isn't there, the bride and the groom must jump over a Dustbuster.

To get a dance with the bride or groom, pin money on the bride's veil or on the groom's suit. A suitable gift is $50, unless you're also hoping for a blow job, in which case you should probably go with a C-note.

Shirts are suggested for the ceremony, but they're optional at the reception. No clothing is expected at the bachelor party, where you will witness ungodly acts of depravity so vile Larry Flynt couldn't imagine them in his most twisted fever dream.

Only the bride, the groom, and one farm animal (of the bride's choosing) are allowed in the honeymoon suite.

Acceptable Gifts for a Cajun Wedding

- Moonshine
- An old boot
- Candlesticks
- Gravel
- A sachet of magic love spices mixed together by a bearded lunatic who lives in the woods

Authentic Cajun Wedding Invitation

Jenny Lou Hennings and
Jimmy Lou Hennings
is pleased to announce
the wedding
of their first mistake, Jackie Lou, to her
cousin and uncle Big Bobby Hennings
on June 28
at the big ol' tree
next to the swamp.

Reception to folla at Johnny Jo's
distillery just over dere yonder
in de bayou.

Overalls required.
Shirts optional.

Some Other Cultural Oddities We Found

• National Hispanic Month is from September 15 to October 15. Apparently, Hispanics thought it only appropriate to start late.

• In the South, the tooth-fairy tradition has a twist: you put money under your pillow and in the morning you wake up to find some teeth.

• The Clip and Dip—a relatively new ceremony for new-borns of mixed Jewish and Christian parents. The festivities involve a "clip" (circumcision) and "dip" (baptism in holy water). This double whammy is guaranteed to turn the kid into a serial killer.

• Allah-ween—a holiday gaining popularity among Muslims living in the Detroit area. On the last night of October, they all go out dressed like terrorists and scare everyone into giving them all their candy, their money, their daughters, and pretty much anything else they want.

• No matter what the guidebooks say, a Texas "hoedown" is not the same as a Baltimore "ho down."

Holidays You Probably Don't Know About, but Should Ask Your Boss for a Day Off Anyway

- Kazimierz Pulaski Day (first Monday in March, Illinois)
- Indigenous Peoples Day (Berkeley, California, on Columbus Day)
- Von Steuben Day (mid-September, German-Americans)
- Woolseymas (December 6. Celebrates Judge Woolsey's decision that *Ulysses* was not pornographic. When they decide it's not boring, we'll read it.)
- Juneteenth (June 19. Honors the end of slavery in the United States. Also, Juneteenth is quite possibly the first word in the history of Ebonics.)

CHAPTER VIII

NAMES AND SLURS

A mericans are obsessed with food. Perhaps it's a result of our native bounty, or that, as a nation, we are simply a gluttonous mass of glucose and fat globules. Another theory held by some is that we've become so loathsome, bloated, and sedated, sex is nowhere near as much fun as hogging down a Dairy Queen sundae.

Whatever the reasons, this food fixation has permeated all the way down into our disparaging descriptions of various ethnic types. Here is a brief sample of some of the food terms used to slam different ethnicities. (Note: this is not a scientific list and leaves out a lot of slurs that we were too lazy or embarrassed to include.)

Oreo—Black on the outside, White on the inside
Eskimo Pie—a ménage à trois with Eskimos
Thin mint—Black with Irish descendants
Apple—American Indian who acts White
Beano—Mexican
Bagel boy—Jew
Ricer—Asian
Cracker—White redneck
Cheesehead—Midwest Caucasian

Pita head—Arab
Mr. Potato Head—Irish male
Aunt Jemima—Large Black woman
Banana—Asian who acts White
Twinkie—also an Asian who acts White
Cashews—offspring of Jew and Catholic
Chocolate dipper—Black man who dates White women
Vanilla swirl—White man who dates Black women
Cookie—Chinese
Egg—White guy dating Asian woman
Eggplant—Italian slur for Blacks
Fig gobbler—Middle Easterner
Heinz—any mixed race
Herring choker—Scandi
KFC—Black
Pancake—Asian
Pizzabagel—Jew/Italian combo
Pork chop—Portuguese
Dandy apple—a gay Indian who acts White

CHAPTER IX

QUIZ

L et's see how much you've learned.

Score Chart
20–23 (answers correct)—potential UN diplomat
15–20—open-minded
5–10—empty-minded
0—future employee of DMV

- Which of the following are Albinos?
    a. Johnny Winter
    b. Edgar Winter
    c. Michael Jackson
    d. Casper the Friendly Ghost

- What is the difference between an Albino and an Albanian?

- How about a Lisbonian and a lesbian?

- If I were a Mormon and had several wives, I'd be called a polygamist. If I were a Black man and had several wives, I'd be called:
  a. A stone-cold pimp
  b. A man about to be stabbed to death by at least one of his wives
  c. The world's first Black Mormon
  d. All of the above

- If I were at my Italian mother's house and I got *scungilli,* I'd have:
  a. Athlete's foot
  b. A venereal disease
  c. Some kind of shellfish
  d. A dream date with Richie Sambora

- *Coolie* refers to:
  a. An Indian yogurt drink
  b. A slur for a Chinese laborer
  c. That has-been rapper with the funny hair

- The percentage of Jews in the NFL is:
  a. 2
  b. 15
  c. 27
  d. 74

- The percentage of Jewish agents of NFL players is:
  a. 97
  b. 98
  c. 99
  d. 100

- *Paneer* means:
  a. "Homosexual" in Spanish
  b. A Cambodian's favorite kind of shoes
  c. An Indian cheese
  d. An Indian's favorite kind of homosexual shoes

- The American city with the fastest-growing Latino population is:
  a. Los Angeles, CA
  b. Bryn Mawr, PA
  c. Flagstaff, AZ
  d. Mexico City, DF

- I went to Passover dinner in Brookline and I wasn't served:
  a. Tzimmes
  b. Gribbens
  c. Haroseth
  d. Chasclkjviuyasktl

• Fill in the blanks:

Paella is to a Spanish-American as _____ is to a Thai-American.
   a. Egg roll
   b. Thai stick
   c. Pad thai
   d. Little boy

If I order pupu, chances are I am _____.
   a. Suffering from an anal fixation
   b. Kosher
   c. Polynesian
   d. Retarded

• "I snizzle your jizzle my nizzle!" means:
   a. I like to drink soda pop from a straw
   b. The euro is at an all-time high against the dollar
   c. No one knows
   d. Actually, we really think that the answer is *b*

• If I am a Cuban-American, I most likely live in:
   a. New York City
   b. South Florida
   c. A 1974 Buick
   d. A constant state of alcohol-fueled rage and denial

- Plantain is to banana as mescal is to . . .
  a. Mescaline
  b. Mueslix
  c. Muslims
  d. Eddie Munster

- Name the ethnic group that boasts the following members:
  a. Mariah Carey
  b. Ryan Seacrest
  c. Supreme Court chief justice John Roberts
  d. SpongeBob SquarePants
  e. Jesse "the Body" Ventura
  f. Since when have these questions had *e*'s and *f*'s?

- If you are at a ceremony and someone smashes a lightbulb, you are:
  a. At a Greenpeace energy summit
  b. At a Jewish wedding
  c. At a Polish electrician's house
  d. About to get gang-raped by Salvadorans

True/False

- At a West Coast Tree Hugger's wedding, the bride and the groom commonly drink each other's urine. (T/F)

- The more elongated eye shape of Asians means they have better peripheral vision, even though they can't drive well. (T/F)

- Fidel Castro's cousin Juan founded the Castro Convertible bed franchise. (T/F)

- Match the following with their definitions:

Macaroon	Good-looking female
Octoroon	Dessert confection
Piece-o'-poon	Of partly Black descent

- Prep-meister Ralph Lauren's real name is:
  a. Ralph Lauren
  b. Ralph Lifshitz
  c. Ralphie Lipschitzkenstein
  d. Betty Friedan
  e. All of the above at one time or another

CHAPTER X

HECHINGER CONVERSION CHART

238

=

AVERAGE WEIGHT
OF ADDISON, OHIO
BOOK CLUB MEMBER

TOTAL NUMBER OF ZOROASTRIANS
LIVING IN THE U.S.

• The average weight of an Addison, Ohio, Women's Book Club member = the number of Zoroastrians currently residing in the United States **(238)**

• The average number of teeth in an Appalachian male's mouth = the number of Jews in the NFL **(4)**

• A Guatemalan-American nanny's yearly income times 250 = a Greenwich Hedge-Fund Manager's monthly stripper budget **($360,000)**

• The number of international Thai movie stars standing on each other's shoulders it takes to equal Shaquille O'Neal **(3)**

- The number of Mennonite females who own bikini tops = the number of South Beach model/actress women who own bikini tops **(0)**

- The number of orgasms in a Jewish woman's life = the number of orgasms Lenny Kravitz had while you were reading that **(3)**

CHAPTER XI

POCKET SURVIVAL GUIDE

This abbreviated guide is meant to be separated at the perforated edges. Then you should laminate it with the lamination kit included in this book packet. Then use the handy ball-bearing necklace (also included in this packet) to hang the laminated pages around your neck so that you'll never be caught without them in a sticky situation. In the unlikely event that the publishers couldn't afford the necklace, the laminating kit, or the perforations, then just tear these pages out and stick them in your pocket. Trust us, you're gonna need them. (If you're of Turkish descent, you may hide these pages in your fez.)

As we've seen by the hundreds of millions of examples included in this book, the chances of running into another ethnic species are high—unless you live in Darien, Connecticut. And even if you live in Darien, you might run across another group while traveling, or perhaps they'll be working on your lawn.

The following is a quick and easy guide to some basics of interethnic interaction. It could save you some embarrassment. It could save your life.

• Only Blacks can use the N-word. Ever. There are no exceptions. There's always at least one White guy in every group who thinks he can get away with using the N-word because he's "down." He is wrong. And you don't want to be around him when he discovers just how wrong he is.

• Anyone can use *spic, kike, guinea,* or *chink,* but it's best to use these words when no spics, kikes, guineas, or chinks are nearby.

• Everyone can always call an Irishman a mick.

• Don't wish Native Americans a "happy Thanksgiving." Turkey makes them sleepy, pumpkin pie makes them sad, and they hate the Cowboys. Frankly, they haven't felt particularly thankful since that whole genocide thing went down.

• Not everyone with a turban is Islamic; some are Hindu, some are Sikh, some are deranged street people with knives and nunchucks hidden under there. Be careful.

• If you hear loud hip-hop bass sounds coming from an approaching car, lock the doors and slink down in your seat. If the approaching car turns out to be filled with suburban White kids with baseball caps on sideways, do not sit up and unlock the doors. Those freaks will shoot you faster than anyone else.

• Old-line WASPs do not think it's funny to joke about how they have lost their mojo in this country. And there's nothing more embarrassing than getting beaten with a penny loafer.

- Not all Latinos are Mexicans. But all Mexicans are Latinos. Either way, none of them like to be referred to as beaners or border bunnies.

- If you notice a young Black man wearing a North Face winter parka in the middle of August, don't assume he has an iron deficiency. Assume he's packing iron.

- Be careful when a tree-hugging, Prius-driving liberal drinks hard liquor at a Planned Parenthood fund-raiser. The drink will go to his head and he will tell offensive, racist jokes until a fistfight breaks out.

- Middle-Aged Asian-American Women (MAAAW) and Young White Teens (YWT) do not use their rearview mirrors for driving. They use them to check their makeup and/or to sing rap lyrics to themselves. In either case, pass them at your earliest convenience.

- Never fight for the last Buffalo chicken wing if you're at a meal with an Extreme Northern New York Sports Fan. You will definitely lose a finger.

- Don't joke around with the Korean restaurant owner and ask him if he has dog on the menu. He just might. And even if he doesn't, you'll never be 100 percent sure.

- Don't be afraid to travel with a Jamaican or Haitian taxi driver who seems high. You should only be afraid if they don't seem high—'cause that's when the accidents happen. Either way, it's going to be a safer ride than if you hailed an angry Pakistani with a Ph.D. who is trying to support twelve people on $40 a day and is still thought of as a terrorist by most of his customers. Our advice: take the bus.

• If you must travel by taxi, definitely avoid the Middle-Aged White Guy with the stained army jacket and the razor stubble who looks as if he's been driving for twelve days straight. And in no circumstances should you go near (or into) his trunk.

Rear-End Identification Tips (REIT)

Not a real estate investment trust, but probably more valuable. Below you'll see several representative derrieres. Being able to identify them from a distance (particularly at night) could mean the difference between life and death.

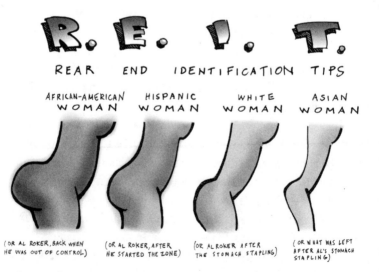

R. E. I. T.

REAR   END   IDENTIFICATION   TIPS

| AFRICAN-AMERICAN WOMAN | HISPANIC WOMAN | WHITE WOMAN | ASIAN WOMAN |

(OR AL ROKER, BACK WHEN HE WAS OUT OF CONTROL)   (OR AL ROKER, AFTER HE STARTED THE ZONE)   (OR AL ROKER AFTER THE STOMACH STAPLING)   (OR WHAT WAS LEFT AFTER AL'S STOMACH STAPLING)

CHAPTER XII

CONCLUSION

The world that our fathers and grandfathers knew is no more. People across the globe communicate instantly via cell phones and the Internet. Plants, animals, and probably people are being cloned as we write this. The Red Sox even stopped choking. It's all very different and a little bit scary.

But the single greatest difference in our world today is us. The people of planet Earth have physically changed more quickly over the past forty years than at any other point in our history. Hell, Cro-Magnon man looks more like Joe McCarthy than Joe McCarthy looks like Kimora Lee Simmons. You know what we mean?

Although we readily admit that the recorded-voice request to "Press one for English" is totally obnoxious, we all have to realize that these changes are for the best. The future is bold and bright and beckoning us from afar. We will embrace the challenges of the years ahead, no longer separated by preposterous, centuries-old ethnic differences. Instead, we will be united by preposterous, brand-new ethnic differences.

We have crisscrossed this great nation from Maine to California and from Florida to the one above Oregon. And we have discovered that this explosion in interethnic commingling has been a wonderful development. (A quick aside to our Appalachian readers—you will note that we refer to a commingling of *ethnicities*, not *species*.)

This mixing up of the ethnic soup has resulted in brilliant and exciting ethnic oddities. But even within ethnicities we have noticed unprecedented varieties that only help to make our national patchwork even more beautiful and patchy.

What will we look like in the future? Many of us will look exactly the same. Many of us will look more and more like our dogs. And according to our computer-generated gene-splicing projections, by the end of the twenty-first century, many of us will look like this: (see facing page)

Hey, we didn't tell you it was pretty, we just told you that it's coming. But there's no need to fear the future, because the present is so darn beautiful. We live in a wonderful country and there's room for everyone here. Even Ling Ling Marcos and his prodigious wanger that he insists on showing to innocent passersby who just want to buy some chardonnay in peace.

It was a great honor for us to finish the work that our grandfather started so many years ago. We're not sure what he hoped or expected to find. But we have drawn a startling conclusion of our own from our hundreds and hundreds of minutes of research:

> The degree to which we are all completely different
> is exactly the same as the degree to which we are all
> exactly the same.

And, with that, we will bid you a fond adieu.

Oh, crap, I think some Jamaicans just broke into our house . . .

THE END

MEET THE WAHJALMI...

7 — 1

3,6,7+1**

1

7

4+5

2

1

5

2

4+5

LOX, SUSHI, ROTI (WITH CHEESE)

(ALL 1-8!)

8

1

2

HORCHICA & TONIC (3,6,+1)

3,6+1*

"WIFE BEATER" POPULAR WITH REDNECKS AS WELL AS 3+6.

1

8

5

** COLIN FARRELL

* 1. WHITE
2. ASIAN
3. HISPANIC
4. JEWISH
5. AFRO
6. LATINO
7. MUSLIM
8. INDIAN

ACKNOWLEDGMENTS

The authors would like to specially thank the illustrator, who wisely chose to remain anonymous. The authors would also like to thank Michele Bové, Claire Dippel, Colin Fox, Lucas Janklow, David Rosenthal, and Adlai Stevenson (not the politician—a different Adlai Stevenson).

ABOUT THE AUTHORS

Kevin and Curtis Hechinger are world-renowned cultural anthro-
pologists. They are also nationally ranked badminton players.
Kevin is an avid fisherman, while Curtis is afraid of the dark. They
are both available for events and parties either as guest speakers
or as just plain guests.